QUANTUM LITE

How to Calm the Chaos

Cover image "Cosmic Evolution Survey ~ Visible Matter
(How cool is that!)
Hubble #STScl-2007-01

The website version of this book was published in 2002 on
www.TheMagicOfQuantum.com by Phyllis Kirk
Quantum Lite was published on Kindle in 2011
ASIN B005FITTH2
Quantum Lite on Create Space/Amazon 2016
ISBN-13:978-1530159918, ISBN-10:1530159911 (color pbk.)
ISBN-13:978-1530350667, ISBN-10:1530350662 (black & white pbk.)

Dedication

to
The Circle of Life

Acknowledgments

With joy and gratitude, I recognize the important people in my life. They have each been my teacher in their own way.

~ Dorothy Mae Olson Kirk for giving me life

~ Robert Winston Kirk for my sense of humor and adventure

~ Ginny and Jan for being my sisters through it all

~ Frank, my mentor, friend and partner

~ Arda, Ali and Abdi Kheyre for being lights in my life

~ Donna for being iridescent

~ Norma,,Colleen and Maggie for being my sisters of choice

~ Lowell for over 5 decades of loyalty to Dorothy and her daughters

~ Dan, Jeff and Grant, each for your unique nephewness

~ Courtney for being my favorite niece

~ Tom, for giving me time and space to grow

~ Ann S, Alice, Katherine, Cate, Deedles, Elizabeth and Nancy for being my sober sisters,

~ Susan, Rhea, Annette, and Liz 'mis hermanas Rincoenas'

~ Eileen Cinque, my Create Space publisher

and

~ Ilya Prigogine for being brilliant, heartful and seeking . . . personifying the balance far from equilibrium.

A special thanks to these members of my website Feedback Team for being early players in the quantum sandbox:

- ~ Jack Rickard
- ~ Tony Loyd
- ~ Tom Doray
- ~ Terry Croskrey
- ~ Kathleen O'Sullivan
- ~ Peggy McAllister
- ~ Jane Kirk
- ~ Barbara and Dan Hutchins
- ~ Maggie Sawada
- ~ Harold Mann

Apology to Grammarians and Theologians

An explanation to the grammarians and theologians of the world: The English teacher in me wants <u>you</u> to know that <u>I</u> know (because I have taught it) and selectively ignore the following:

~ One should never use a preposition to end a sentence with :)

~ Numbers under 10 should be spelled, not giving their numeric symbol;

~ It is proper to say 'to whom', 'from whom', 'with whom', etc.;

~ Fragments are unacceptable;

~ Contractions shouldn't be used in formal writing;

~ . . . and all the other rules that standardize the English language.

And I want you to know that I know that I use 'their' instead of 'his/her', and 'they' instead of 'she/he', etc. I admit to playing fast and loose with quotations, freely replacing 'he', 'him' and 'Man' with' they', 'them' and 'One'

You won't find God referred to as He (or She, It or They), and rarely as God. I agree with Bucky Fuller (of geodesic dome fame) that the word God has become anthropomorphic – it makes God into our own image. Bucky used Greater Intelligence, Greater Integrity and Universe. For me, the jury is still out on what God is, so I use words that support that exploration. Einstein's 'Whatever' is definitely vast enough. I like what the Australian Aborigines have been using for 50,000 years: Divine Oneness. Other words that offer the right feeling are: Source, Consciousness and All That Is.

Before I began writing, I pondered my writing style. One academician with whom (See? I know) I had had a stimulating conversation said, "And your book will be well annotated, of course?" To which I replied, "Of course." But I had to admit that my heart wasn't in it. I didn't want to grind away at a scholarly tome that sought to appeal only to the intellectual elite.

My goal is to create a book that is 'available' and 'readable'. I want my book to be conversational, understandable and enjoyable. I believe that 'thought-provoking' can also be humorous. As a matter of fact, the brain learns better when it is entertained. Children laugh a lot when they are learning naturally. I have made this book as interactive as possible because the brain remembers better when more senses are involved. You'll find that the calm music (if you're on the website) helps slow the heart and make the brain more receptive. (If you're not on the website, play Baroque in the background for yourself.)

My first guideline is to make the book simple, direct and clear. Mark Twain said to a friend, "I'd have written you a shorter letter, but I didn't have the time." I am finding how true that is. All eleven planned chapters of this book were drafted over a decade ago on St. Vincent's Island. As I now prepare the Kindle version of my web book of five chapters and a Review, I am amazed at how long it takes to write simply and clearly, especially for a lawyer. I know I haven't arrived yet.

So grammarians of the world, please know that I respect our craft. Know that when I take short-cuts, they are mostly conscious ones. They are made in the interest of inclusion (the positive word for non-sexist) and a conversational style. I trust that the trade-off is worth it.

Preface to Third Edition

It's been over 10 years since I published <u>The Magic of Quantum</u> on my website with moving graphics and music. It's been 5 years since I renamed it <u>Quantum Lite</u> and put it on Kindle. Now I get to birth it in hard copy on Amazon.

My last 10 years of deepening experience (participating in chaos) echoes what Hildegard of Bingen knew in 1200:

Live your life

on the green, growing edges

of becoming.

It is only fear that hinders us from doing this. I believe we are on the edge of beginning to learn how to live the glorious lives we have been gifted ~ without fear. It will be the hardest work the human race has done. We have the tools and the knowledge to do it. Do we have the will and the wisdom to make the choices that can move us as a species into lives of exploration and creativity in a world that works for everyone? What an adventure. And we're here for it. Wahoo!

"The following message applies to all souls everywhere.

You are a spiritual being here on earth having a Human experience.

You elected to come.

It was not an accident nor by chance that you were born of the two people who are your biological parents.

You were aware of who they were, of the circumstances under which you were conceived and the inherent genetic pattern of both. You said, 'Yes!'

Your being here is voluntary, self-assigned, and long-awaited."

Message From Forever by Marlo Morgan quoting 50,000-year-old Australian Aboriginal wisdom

Table of Contents

F0RWARD

First, I will tell you how I got into quantum, or rather, how quantum got into me. Then, the thesis of Quantum Lite (the what and why). Next you will get a very simplified explanation of quantum. Then, the chaos model that explains it all. At the end of the book in the Epilogue is my briefest, bestest wisdom on how to calm the chaos by transforming fear.

How Quantum Entered My Life

I remember lying awake at night as a child wondering what was on the other side of the edge of the universe. If the universe was expanding, what was it expanding into? What is nothingness like? What was beyond the nothingness?

My first real teacher in this kind of thinking was my Uncle Fred. He was married to my mother's youngest sister Henrietta and they farmed in western Kansas. They were both pilots. Uncle Fred was a HAM radio operator and played a mean clarinet. Despite the fact that he'd never been to college, my Uncle Fred was the smartest person I knew. And he treated me like an adult. We had wonderful conversations about things that were never talked about in school. Like the edge of the universe. I remember Uncle Fred answering my questions one time by saying that there are things that we as humans don't have the capacity to comprehend. "It's like putting a dog at a podium and expecting him to deliver a speech. It's beyond the dog's capacity to do that. We're like the dog. We just don't have the capacity to understand what's on the other side of the edge of the universe." I liked the analogy, but didn't like the answer.

This book is an attempt to find my own authentic answers. Not someone else's based on second-hand research. At this point in my life, I want my answers based on my own experience. My questions have changed. I'm no longer plagued by what's beyond the edge. Now what I want to know is "How does it all work?" I have experienced a flow, a rhythm that is there - available - even in the chaos. I have begun consciously experimenting with my own life, paying acute attention to what happens when the input varies, goes 'beyond my control'.

My real question is "How do I get it all to work for me?" It's a self-centered control thing, I'm sure. Based on my objective observation of my own life (if that's possible), I can say that my life has continued to get better over the years. My life now is sprinkled with moments of happiness and extended periods of deep satisfaction. Perhaps this is simply the wisdom of age. On the other hand, perhaps I really am getting some things figured out about the Big Picture. And in <u>Quantum Lite</u> I'm sharing it to see if it works beyond my own little Petri dish . . . and maybe to find like-minded explorers who are discovering their piece to the puzzle that might work for me. And because it jazzes me when something I write has meaning for someone else – confirming the big poster made by Frank (you'll meet him soon) that "It's all relationships."

I had an image in a dream once. In the dream, I was floating in from outer space through the galaxy, towards home. In the vastness, on my right there was a large clear flat circular field with a few simple geometric figures in it: lines, long thin U-shaped figures, a few dots. They were moving. Then I saw that it was made up of two planes, like two clear flat glass plates on top of each other. The same geometric patterns were on both plates. The bottom plate was at rest. The top plate was rotating clockwise. As I watched, the two sets of figures moved into alignment with each other. I literally "felt" it click into place like a soft sonic boom had encompassed me. *

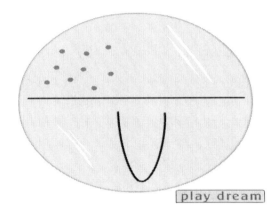

play dream

*To see moving graphics and hear sound, go to
www.themagicofquantum.com, click Read the Book, and go to
Foreword.

Interestingly enough, this dream came to me in my mid-forties, around the time I met Frank and quantum. It is quantum physics that has given me the context to align the realities of my life in a way that made sense to me – put the pieces in place, so to speak.

Quantum emerged for me at Sundance, Utah. The flood of information that triggered <u>Quantum Lite</u> began there. Or maybe eons before that, but in limited reality, it was at the Sundance conference that the lightening struck.

My mentor, friend and partner Frank Clement was with me. Frank had spent thirty years as a scientist at Bell Labs, and had invented both the Speakerphone and the Touch Screen Computer. When Frank retired from Bell Labs, he had started the Boulder Center of Accelerative Learning, Inc. (BCAL). That way, he could play around with thinking and creativity, call it corporate training and get paid for it!

Frank Clement at a BCAL workshop

So there we were at the Sundance conference. Frank was excited about sitting at the feet of Fritjof Capra, the famous physicist. I was eager to meet Meg Wheatley, the pioneer in applying quantum thought to corporations. It was Dr. Margaret Wheatley's Self-Organizing Systems Conference at Robert Redford's ski resort & independent film festival center outside of Salt Lake City, Utah. It was the winter of l996.

My soul caught fire at this conference. I was in the company of Fritjof and Meg, and learning about the work of Dr. Ilya Prigogine (Pre' go jean). A passion ignited in me for the quantum world and its possibilities. It was a peak experience where my mind kept exploding with Aha's.

My first day back in Boulder, I sat at my desk. I was eager to translate what I was beginning to understand about quantum as a result of Dr. Prigogine's Theory of Dissipative Structures. It had won him the Nobel Prize in chemistry in 1977. A central theme of his work was chaos. His theory proved that earth wasn't headed for a heat death (as the Second Law of Thermodynamics implies). Instead, his theory showed that the result of chaos can be just the opposite of death and disintegration. He proved that chaos can create a higher energy level that is better equipped to handle more activity and more chaos. The little word that caught my attention was 'can'.

Frank, my teacher in so many areas, had taught me the value of putting complex concepts into simple models. As I stared at a blank piece of paper in front of me, a model began forming in my mind. I drafted my first Model of Dissipative Structures: simple lines, arrows, waves. With excitement (and some fear of rejection), I went to Frank's office to show him. He liked it! Frank's enthusiasm for the model was all the affirmation I needed.

I daringly called it the Kirk Model of Dissipative Structures. Frank's use of his own name in the Clement Bubble Theory of the Mind gave me courage. Right up front here, I want to give credit to the other two co-creators: Dr. Prigogine, of course; and the Whatever that did a fly-by that morning and dropped it into my awareness. The model evolved into the Kirk Model of Chaos (KMC).

Frank and I introduced the KMC in a new workshop on self-organizing systems, called Quantum Leadership. We were pleased to see how people responded to the model, and how profound their resulting insights were.

But the real test was the scrutiny of the author of the theory, Dr. Prigogine himself. The idea of showing the model to Dr. Prigogine germinated gradually. (Frank had made his transition and gone to play with Bucky, Isaac Asimov and Gene Rodenberry in the Whatever. He had died on Cinco de Mayo, May 5, 1997, only 6 months after discovering his cancer.) The following spring, an ad for a conference called The Paradox of Certainty caught my eye. It was to be held in Austin, Texas with Prigogine as the keynote speaker. The registration was expensive, but the lure of actually sitting in the same room with Dr. Prigogine had me hooked.

"I'll be able to tell people what he's like, how it feels to 'be in his energy'," as one says in Boulder. I felt the expense was justified. Then one day I thought, "Why not arrange to meet him? It would definitely vindicate the cost (and inflate my ego) if I could casually drop his name in the workshops like, "When I met Dr. Prigogine . . ." So I began planning how to meet him personally. I began envisioning being able to shake his hand and thank him for his contribution of the Theory of Dissipative Structures . . . maybe even tell him how effective it was in our workshops. Then on a day when my biorhythms were on high. I said, "What the h---! You might as well show him your model."

On April 15, 1998, I found myself in Texas, walking across the lawn at Austin's Lake Way Inn, doing focused breathing to quell my terror. Within an hour, after his talk, I'd have my private audience with Dr. Prigogine. Every fear demon I had was raging. "Who in the world do you think you are? Fritjof Capra has just introduced Dr. Prigogine as being on par with Einstein, and you haven't had physics since high school! You're being way too arrogant here. You're wasting the time of a very important man. You'll embarrass yourself. You'll be humiliated. What if he destroys my model? What if he laughs at it?" I felt like the mother watching her baby suspended under Solomon's sword.

© 2002 by Linda S. Nis
(Spanish Moss)

I stopped on the grass to calm myself. There was a beautiful gray-green fuzzy clump of Spanish moss that had fallen at my feet from the tree above.

I looked around. No other clumps of moss lying anywhere around. I bent over and picked it up with a little smile, feeling as if the Whatever had dropped it there to get me to lighten up. I reminded myself that I had seen the effect of the KMC on others for 2 years. As scared as I was of having it discredited, this was the ultimate test, and I wanted to know. Silently, I went through the 4 touchstones I use when I'm really unsure of myself:

~ Am I showing up with my unique voice?

Yes, definitely.

~ Am I speaking my truth without judgment?

Yes.

~ Am I paying attention to what has heart and meaning for me?

Yes.

~ Am I letting go of the outcome?

No. I was very invested in Dr. Prigogine liking my model.

What would letting go feel like? It would mean staying totally open to his response, being willing to change the model, even throw it away.

I told myself that no matter what happened, my family would still love me. Life would go on even in the worst case scenario if he destroyed my model. I took a few more slow breaths and then I continued walking to the conference room. I felt willing to accept whatever was on its way. I could trust that whatever happened, in the long run, would be beneficial for me.

I sat through Dr. Prigogine's lecture, hanging on every word, understanding little. Because my years in Russia gave me a familiarity with his accent, I got his words, but only vaguely got his concepts. His work on Probability and the Arrow if Time was and still is, beyond me. But I felt delicious things rolling around in my brain. They were not making contact enough to find meaning. More like pin balls bouncing off of bells and buzzers, throwing out sparks of light and sound.

These are the jewels from my notes:

~ probability as the central element of quantum and classical mechanics

   ~ chaos's sensitivity to initial conditions

      ~ vibration to rotation

~ the evolution of humanity is the evolution of communication

   ~ chaos/dynamics of correlation

      ~ <u>trajectory</u> or location, not both

         ~ nature uses irreversibility to produce life

~ Einstein to Van Gogh, "Ask the moon why it moves."

   ~ determinism vs. thermodynamics

      ~ Laplace's demon = Fate

         ~ the end of certainty: time, chaos and new laws of nature

~ Classical periodicity. Now, time fluidity.

   ~ Poincare . . . Niels Bohr . . . Karl Popper . . . Jules Henri

      ~ *Empire of Chance* by Gerd Gigerenzer

         ~ equilibrium is reached at maximum of entropy

~ Most phenomenon on earth are irreversible, so Newtonian classical mechanics applies to a very small part

   ~ near equilibrium is positive feedback

(therefore far from equilibrium = negative feedback??)

~ fusion is decisions at the top . . . fission is
    decisions at the bottom

~ uncertainty needs more choices

~ the sun's flow creates non-equilibrium state
    on our earth

~ A town is a structure. It is involved in a
    flow of energy in and out.

~ Adam Smith's 'invisible hand' in economics is the
    self-regulating aspect of living systems

~ Humanity is a relationship history, not a study
    of Robinson Crusoes.

~ In early studies, he analyzed traffic:

> the individual regime;

> the collective regime;

> where you drive others
    and others drive you.

~ Principle of quantum mechanics: wave function in
    a world of possibilities . . . when we
    measure, we collapse the wave.

~ We are participating: The mechanics of
    bifurcation is different in humans than
    bifurcation in molecules because we
    humans compare what is to what can be.
    This suggests we choose.

~ Do we choose based on behavior before
bifurcation or at bifurcation?

~ The Nobels voted that science is not a danger.
The optimists won.

By the end of Prigogine's talk, my brain was
hyperventilating. I had worked hard to follow his line of
thought. At the same time, I wanted to capture the
explosions going on in my brain. I wanted to follow all the

trails shooting out from the chain reactions.

Dr. Prigogine's quiet closing comment won my heart. He said, "Understanding this gives us the energy to try to participate in creation."

Dr. Ilya Prigogine
Nobel Prize Laureate in Chemistry 1977

I felt excited and ready to meet him. The twenty minutes he granted me felt like a timeless moment. As I walked him through my chaos model on two large easels, his comments were direct and instructive. At the end, he asked me if I had published, which caught me by surprise. He asked me to write to him. I assured him I would.

As I walked out with Dr. Prigogine, I felt blessed by the presence of this brilliant, humble, focused man. I felt at peace, elated and excited about the door that had opened for me to participate in creation. This book is the result of walking through that door.

Thesis of
<u>Quantum Lite</u>

<u>Quantum Lite</u> begins with an explanation of quantum chaos. Chapters 1 - 3 give you and understanding of energy, systems and chaos theory from a quantum perspective. Chaos Theory tells us that chaos is a constantly

recurring function of a healthy system. (That's the bad news.) The rest of the book is how to stay happy during chaos. (That's the good news.) This is quantum reality that offers a way to *'be '* in chaos without *'being in chaos'*.

(Really) Basic Comparison of
Newtonian Physics and Quantum Physics

Newtonian Physics (also called Classical Physics) is named after Isaac Newton. He was the brilliant scientist who lived in the late 1600's. His thinking shaped the next 300 years of history.

Sir Isaac Newton at age 47

By watching an apple fall from a tree, Newton came up with 3 laws of motion. His laws tell us how we can predict. (prediction) If you take an apple that weighs 'X' and you throw it with force 'Y' at an angle of 'Z' , then it will land right over there at point 'A'. We can predict outcomes because we know the elements of force, angle, and weight. Things can be determined. (determinism) Everything can be reduced to parts and pieces. (reductionism) Once you know the piece and force, it follows a set line of travel. (linear) Cause and effect (causality) are all there is. And the god of this world is the Scientific Method. It says that whatever is true can be objectively observed (objectivism), and can be repeated and measured. It says that there are two separate sources (duality): me as the observer, and the thing I am looking at. (observer/observed) In Newtonian Physics, the earth is like a windup clock and the universe is a huge machine. (mechanistic) We can use force to manipulate desired outcomes. We humans are in control, and all is right with the world.

Enter quantum. Quantum Physics says, "Yes, Newtonian Physics is true in limited circumstances. Newton's laws still apply, but not everywhere. We have discovered the next level of reality, and it looks really strange." Some of the world's greatest minds came together in 1927 to struggle with this new reality

The Birth of Quantum Physics ~
The 1927 Solvay physics conference in Brussels Belgium
Some of the really big names in quantum (most of whom were at this conference) that you'll want to at least recognize are: Einstein (you'll see his bushy head in the front row center), Heisenberg (of the Uncertainty Principle), Niels Bohr, Pauli, Max Born, Schrödinger (of Schrödinger's Cat), David Bohm, Feynman, Mandelbrot, and Max Plank.

These scientists were looking at a new reality that was vastly different from Newton's physics. Imagine a tiny cup (the kind they serve that really strong coffee in). Now take a huge soup pot and set the cup inside it. Inside that cup is the world of Newtonian Physics, and Newtonian laws apply. The space outside the cup is the world of Quantum Physics. A different set of laws applies here.

In the quantum soup pot things get really weird. You cannot predict where something will be just by knowing its size, path and force. (indeterminism) Things don't travel in a direct line. (non-linearity) They disappear from here and instantly appear somewhere else *without going through the space in between. . . .* sort of like time travel. And speaking of time, it doesn't really exist – except inside its own local region of reality, the little cup. One thing can be in two forms. It is both a wave of energy and a particle of matter. (wave/particle duality) And forget cause and effect. Things happen seemingly without cause (acausality) and by chance (random).

In Quantum Physics, the proton, neutron and electron are no longer the smallest pieces of matter. We now have cool-sounding things like quarks (and anti-quarks), quasars, pi-mesons, hadrons, leptons. And the smallest pieces we are finding are not solid pieces; they are bundles of invisible energy. There's the String Theory that says that within our 3-dimensional world there are other hidden dimensions. What would a world of 10 or more dimensions look like? How do you collapse extra dimensions into a 3-D reality so they exist in the same space?

The word 'quantum' comes from the word for 'quantity' or 'how much'. Max Plank talked about how energy can only be absorbed, or move, in tiny, separate packets. If you want a very easy to read, in-depth explanation about anything quantum, get <u>Who's Afraid of Schrodinger's Cat? An A-to-Z Guide to All the New Science Ideas You Need to Keep Up with the New Thinking</u> by Ian Marshall and Danah Zohar. It's the CliffsNotes of quantum.

Quantum Quiz

Below is a fun comparison of Newtonian and Quantum adapted and enhanced from the work of Meg Wheatley and Myron Kellner-Rogers. See if you can fill in the blanks (See complete chart at end of Foreword.) Take the Newtonian concept on the left, go directly across to the right column and expand it to a quantum concept.

Newtonian	Quantum
Matter is made up of 'things'	Matter is bundles of energy in relationship to each other
The world is a clockwork machine	The world is _____
We understand things by taking them apart	We understand things by _____
Knowledge comes in pieces: science, math, art	Knowledge is seamless
People have narrow, specific skills	People _____
Motivation is based on manipulation of external lures	Motivation is based on _____ _____
Things fall apart	Things _____
The basic unit is 'things'	Relationships are all there is
Structures are man-made	Structure _____
Order comes from having structure	Order comes from freedom of information

Information should be closely managed	Information should be open, abundant
Either/or	_____
Certainty	Inconsistency
Predictable	_____
Determined	Undeterminable
Linear	Non-linear
Observer/Observed	Participant
Duality: good/bad; right/wrong	_____
Judgment and exclusion	Perception and choice
Change is the troubling exception	Change is _____
We want equilibrium	We want to be at the edge of chaos

At this point, you may take comfort in the words of Niels Bohr, one of the big names in quantum. He says, "If you're not in awe, you don't understand quantum." Awe is what I felt at Sundance. (This is not to imply that therefore, I understand quantum.)

This book is my explanation of how quantum can show up in life day-to-day . . . how I can use quantum to enrich my life. For example, if there really are multiple realities, how can I access those other realities and what can they do for me? What's the "So what?" of all this for me – here and now at this moment in my life?

You will not find lots of science. That's why it's titled Quantum Lite. This book is the experiential side of the scientific. It is my search for how to make use of what science tells us is reality. If it's real, then it is available to me, even if it's an alternate reality that appears magical. How do I access it? What can it do for me?

Quantum Lite is my explanation of how I have chosen to live in a world of uncertainty, of probabilities, of multiple realities, of radical, non-linear explosions. Seen through Newtonian glasses, that world can be terrifying, life-sucking and depressing because I'm not in control. Seen through quantum eyes, that same world is delightful, entertaining and life-giving because I am abundantly supported by my participation and my belonging.

Newtonian Quantum Answer Key

(aka the Cheat Sheet)

Newtonian	Quantum
Matter is made up of 'things'	Matter is bundles of energy in relationship to each other
The world is a clockwork machine	The world is a great thought
We understand things by taking them apart	We understand things by looking at the whole
Knowledge comes in pieces: science, math, art	Knowledge is seamless
People have narrow, specific skills	People learn continually
Motivation is based on manipulation of external lures	Motivation is based on a person's connection to the whole
Things fall apart	Things self-organize
The basic unit is 'things'	Relationships are all there is
Structures are man-made	Structure emerges
Order comes from having structure	Order comes from freedom of information

Information should be closely managed	Information should be open, abundant
Either/or	Both/and
Certainty	Inconsistency
Predictable	Random
Determined	Undeterminable
Linear	Non-linear
Observer/Observed	Participant
Duality: good/bad; right/wrong	Wholism: it all belongs
Judgment and exclusion	Perception and choice
Change is the troubling exception	Change is all there is
We want equilibrium	We want to be at the edge of chaos

Chapter 1

Einstein and Astrology

I am sitting at my desk in my fifth grade homeroom in Longmont, Colorado. It's 1958. Miss Mattison has just handed out the new My Weekly Reader. I look down at an explosive picture of Albert Einstein's bushy hair and intense eyes. Under the picture in large print Einstein is saying:

"It's all energy.

Everything is energy

Everything."

The room fades and dissolves around me. I am transfixed by Einstein's face and the revelation that has just burned itself into my brain -- rearranging my reality forever. I don't remember a thing the article said. I don't remember if I even understood any of it. This turning point in my life, significant as it was, didn't lead me into the sciences. Science never called to me the way the world of words, people, the mind called to me. The various major attractions in my undergrad and post-grad years were psychology, English literature, political science, education, law.

It wasn't until early adulthood that science again intruded into my liberal arts world. My social conscience, sense of adventure, and need to have a job had led me to be a teacher at Wendell Phillips High School in Chicago's south side ghetto. One day I was walking down the deserted hallway after school with a science teacher who I really admired.

Darrell Spense was a tall, thoughtful man who seemed to carry himself above the politics and cliques of Wendell Phillips.

I wanted to be sure that Darrell knew I was really intelligent despite the fact that I was teaching EMH (educable mentally handicapped). So in response to his mention of one of our colleagues, I said "I don't know her very well. We have the same lunch break, but she sits at the table with the group that reads their horoscopes during lunch." I rolled my eyes in what I hoped was tastefully subtle arrogance.

Darrell said nothing for a few steps. Then, quietly, "I take it you don't believe in astrology." I was dumbstruck. There was no one I respected more on the entire staff than Darrell. A science teacher, and he's implying that he believes in that ridiculous stuff.

Darrell continued in his thoughtful objective tone, "So tell me about the tides, Phyllis.

What causes the tides?"

"The moon, of course."

"How does the moon do it?" he pressed.

"Well, some kind of magnetic attraction," I answered, sensing he was going somewhere with his line of questions.

"How far away is it? How big is it?"

"I don't know," I admitted, not feeling persuasively brilliant.

"Well," Darrell explained, "It's about one-quarter the size of the Earth, and about one-quarter million miles away. It's a chunk of cold rock. Yet it pulls and pushes the oceans of this planet with a force and regularity that we still don't completely understand."

"If a hunk of dead rock can affect our planet that strongly, how much more affect could an entire constellation of live stars have?" he reasoned.

We were in Darrell's corner classroom by now, the late afternoon sun finding its way through the grimy windows. "Do you know about the Electromagnetic Spectrum?" "No," I said, feeling confused. But I was intrigued enough to let go of some of my pretense in the light of Darrell's quiet, rational approach.

He walked me to a wall poster with a series of different colors fanning out in a semi-circle. "This is the entire range of electrical and magnetic radiation we know of at this point. It ranges from these gamma rays on the right hand side of the spectrum with a wavelength of one one-hundredth of an angstrom. An angstrom is one ten millionth of a meter."

"Smaller than a virus. Real small."

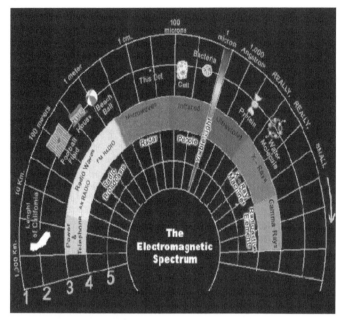

1 ~ Wavelength in meters

2 ~ Size of Wavelength

3 ~ Common name of wave

4 ~ Source of Wavelength

5 ~ Frequency (waves per second)

Then he pointed to the left side of the spectrum. "At the other end here are waves with spans the length of California."

"And this," he said as he pointed to a tiny rainbow about a half inch wide at the top right, "is all the human eye can see. Of this entire spectrum, only this miniscule amount is made up of frequencies that the eye can respond to."

"Now all these," he ran his hand over the rest of the spectrum, "are real, scientific, useable. We can't see radio waves, or infrared rays (though dogs can!), or X-rays, or microwave. But they are very, very real. They are simply non-physical. What we can see, the physical, is a very small part of the real world."

I studied the ELM Spectrum for a minute. Interesting. This chart represented all the energy we knew about the world. Somewhere up around the rainbow of visible light, I noticed with surprise that 'People' were a source of energy.

"Have you ever heard of Bucky Fuller?"

I shook my head. It sounded like a football player I should know.

"Bucky Fuller is a brilliant engineer who designed the geodesic dome, among other things. Bucky says 99.9% of all reality is invisible."

"The reason for this, come to think of it," Darrell mused, "might be because most energy frequencies are invisible. You know, everything is energy. Everything is made up of energy." A chill went down my back as the memory of my grade school classroom came back.

Darrell then proceeded to give me the rational understanding of Einstein's proclamation that had affected me so deeply in grade school.

"At the leading edge of science, researchers now are going deep into sub-atomic particles to find the smallest particle of matter. It used to be the atom, then the 'quark'. Now, what they are finding is that the smallest particles aren't particles at all. They're bundles of information and energy swirling around each other. Matter, at its core, isn't matter. It is energy. It's all energy. Everything is energy."

"So. Back to astrology. It may be an unproven science, but just because we can't prove or explain invisible energy doesn't mean we can't use it. Even Einstein couldn't explain gravity. But," and here Darrell bent his knees and sprang into the air, "every time I jump up, gravity pulls me back down," and he landed, raising a puff of dust around his feet.

"Just like gravity, someday we may be able to explain how and why astrology works. But now, for me, it's enough to know there's some rational basis for it, and I'm open to the help it can give me." Then he threw back his head as if an idea had just struck him, and laughing, he said, "You know who Alexander Graham Bell was, right?"

Yes, on this one.

"Well, one of my favorite mind-ahead-of-its-time stories is about Bell. He had perfected the telephone to the point where he was ready to introduce it to the public. He had set up a demonstration in a three story building in downtown New York. He had a speaker and receiver on the first floor connected to a speaker and receiver on the third floor. He had invited the press, dignitaries and some benefactors. Uninvited to the party came members of the NYPD. They came with an arrest warrant for Alexander Graham Bell on charges of seeking to defraud the public. . . "Because," and here he raised his eyebrows and nose, changing to a conceited tone, "everyone knows that the human voice cannot travel over pieces of barn wood and wire!"

I laughed. I could picture the scene.

"You know, something as simple as TV would have been magic even a hundred years ago." Darrell chuckled. "If we brought back Newton, one of the brightest minds of the seventeenth century, and put him in front of a Sony color TV, he'd probably take off screaming 'Witchcraft!'"

When I left Darrell's classroom that day, I was a different person. The real world had changed shape. From then on, there were two types of reality for me. One was the physical reality, or things I could see and touch. The other was the non-physical, a reality that I slowly began experiencing without the use of the five senses. It was those things I couldn't see or touch that were just as real and useful such as radio waves, and perhaps even astrology.

Harmony and the Void

I am eighteen years old and traveling with the international singing cast of "Up With People". My cast is performing in Chicago. I am with a few other cast members at Chicago's landmark Palmer House. I'm standing at the lobby elevator waiting to go up. The doors open, and I hear two amazed voices saying "Why, it's Phyllis!" "Is that you, Phyllis?" I am looking into the faces of Mildred and Avery Caldwell, family friends from my hometown of Longmont, Colorado, over a thousand miles, and several light-years, away.

Mildred and Avery Caldwell belong to the same church as my family, and their two sons, John and Tom, are the ages of my sister Jan and me. Tom and I had dated some in high school. Even more amazing now in retrospect, is the fact that Tom and I were married twelve years after this incident.

How can we explain this kind of 'coincidence'? Mildred, Avery and I were all just passing through Chicago, a city of millions of people and thousands of buildings. What on earth brought us face-to-face at just that moment in time and at just that spot? Most of you have experienced similar amazing coincidences, too amazing to be totally random and totally accidental.

For years this occurrence nagged me. I, like Einstein, do not believe God plays dice with the Universe. It was not a crap shoot that collided the Caldwells and me in Chicago. Only recently have I found an explanation that satisfies me.

'Synchronicity' is what Carl Jung called this. 'Two seemingly unrelated events, unconnected by obvious cause and effect, yet unquestionably linked.' Two obviously connected events coinciding in time and space without a scientifically explainable basis. Enter the Darrel Spense Principle: accept it, seek to understand it, but most importantly, use it if it serves you. After years of pondering and probing for possible rationale, I have arrived at an understanding of synchronicity that satisfies me.

Whether Carl Jung was aware of it or not, his psychological concept of (synchronous) has a very illuminating definition in the electromagnetic world. 'Synchronous' in physics and electricity means 'having the same frequency and zero phase difference.' Roughly translated, synchronous means two things are vibrating at the same rate. They are on exactly the same wavelength.

Since everything is energy, we human beings are energy. Each of us is a condensed, consolidated bundle of millions of energy waves. That bundle is dense enough and vibrating slowly enough to be in the physical, and therefore, visible to the eye.

Think of the human body as a big radio wave. It's like a radio wave that comes into your TV. One small wave enters, but it translates into dozens of channels. That one small radio wave contains oodles (to use a scientific term) of smaller frequencies. Just so, the human body's wave length contains millions of different frequencies, or waves.

Very simplified, the human body's cluster of wavelengths looks something like this:

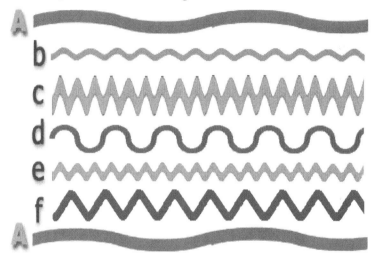

This model shows only a few wavelengths to give you the idea. In reality, there are millions of wavelengths vibrating in our bodies. The broad outside wave, 'A', is the blended sum total of all the millions of separate frequencies inside you. 'A' is what I look like to the world: a 54-year-old female writer living in Puerto Rico, picking up sea glass to entertain herself.

Every experience a person has literally leaves its energetic mark on them in the form of a new wavelength. Think of an experience that you had recently. That experience was like an immersion of your body in a field or pool of the specific energetic frequency of that event, place or person. (I use 'frequency', 'wave' and 'wavelength' interchangeably.) When you had that experience, your body absorbed that frequency. A new wavelength has been born in your body that now contains that same frequency as the field of experience you were just in. This is one way magnets are made. A piece of non-magnetic metal is left in the magnetic field of a magnet until its wavelengths are aligned with the magnet's wavelengths. It is then magnetized.

Your parents may have lived through the Depression, World War I or II, the Roaring 20's, Amelia Earhart's flights. So their bodies carry a Depression frequency, a Roaring 20's frequency, an Amelia Earhart frequency. If you were alive when Sputnik went up, when Kennedy was shot, when Neil Armstrong walked on the moon, when Gandhi made his Salt March, when Challenger exploded, you have a Sputnik, a Kennedy, a Challenger, a Gandhi frequency in you. Or HarryPotter or Star Wars . . .

The strength of that frequency ('amperage' in electrical terms), depends on how long or how strong your immersion was in the field. I had lived in Longmont half my life, so when I was 18 and ran into the Caldwells in Chicago, my Longmont frequency was very strong. The few seconds it took for the news of Kennedy's death to envelope me wasn't long, but it was intense. And as long as I live, I will remember feeling the people of the world rejoice as we watched the Berlin Wall come down in 1989. All these experiences left strong frequencies in me.

Look back at the illustration above of the human body's frequency. The 'b' frequency in me is the wave that was born in me by living in Longmont, Colorado from fourth grade through college. Everyone who's lived in Longmont has a similar 'Longmont' wave in them. Mildred and Avery had the 'Longmont' wavelength in them. It was the magnetic attraction of those identical waves that drew us to be at the elevator door of the Palmer House at the same moment. The same frequency and the same phase vibration of our identical Longmont, Colorado wavelengths attracted us to the 'synchronous' event of colliding with each other in a time and space of unlimited variables and infinite possibilities.

The 'c' frequency is my 'Scott' wave. My first home was Scott City, Kansas. I lived in Scott City from birth until age three, then again from age seven to nine. All of my father's family was in Scott City where Grandmother Della and Granddad JE lived, raised wheat and nine children. 'Scott' is an important frequency for me. Over the years, I've noticed that the Scotts that have come into my life have been major positive influences. Scott Klososky and I met in Moscow. We formed Matrix, Inc., which became the U.S. partner in Paragraph, our Soviet American Joint Venture. Our Soviet partners in Paragraph were some of my strongest and most helpful friends during my 'challenging' three years in Moscow. I eventually profited when Silicon Graphics International bought Paragraph. Scott and I have remained friends, though no longer business partners. He continues to be a delightful and helpful person in my life.

During my years as head of BCAL, Scott Allen was a generous and supportive person. During those same years, Scott Robinson (the former partner of my colleague and close friend Colleen Schreiner) was also a steadfast friend. Now, when a Scott shows up in my life, I pay attention. I don't put expectations on them, but I simply turn up my awareness and stay tuned for the possibilities.

The 'd' frequency could be my 'quantum' frequency. It riveted my fifth grade mind, it drew me to Darrell Spense, it attracted me to Frank Clement (the scientist inventor who became my partner), it attracted Frank and me to Meg Wheatley and Fritjof Capra, it helped me understand Prigogine's work and create the chaos model from it, it drew me to meet Dr. Prigogine himself. It attracted you to this book.

Many of you have experienced synchronicity. Have you ever walked into a party that's a room full of strangers? Then, the first person you meet as you're grazing at the buffet, trying to look comfortable, turns out to be someone who went to the same high school you did, or who knows your favorite maiden aunt in Buffalo, or who absolutely hated the same movie you did that everyone else is raving about?

These events are connected. The laws of energy explain why.

Spend a few minutes with the model below. Describe what 'A', your exterior physical body, looks like to the world. What are five adjectives that describe you?

"I am……" and list five adjectives (descriptive words) that express you.

What are five verbs that describe you?

"I ......" and list five verbs (action words) that describe you.

Now think about what wavelengths you have inside you. Clue: What patterns show up repeatedly in your life: what kind of people; what places; what events?

What could be frequency 'b' in you?

What could be frequency 'c'?

What is frequency 'd'?

Understanding these basics of how energy works in our lives is an important step in understanding how chaos works within quantum.

When I was a trial lawyer with the Solicitor's Office, I got to spend time with an enlightening electrical master. Dr. John White was my electrical expert on a trial in Utah. I still remember my 'Dinner with John'. He was highly experienced, thoughtful and objective, a very desirable expert witness. Although he'd been a student of electricity his whole life, he was still mystified by it, almost reverent about it. John said, "We don't really understand the very basics of electricity. It's predictable and consistent. We know it always seeks to return to its source the easiest way possible, the path of least resistance. But we don't know why. We don't really know why." (I could hear Darrell Spence chuckling!)

Energy seeks completion. There are two ways that energy completes itself. The first way is through harmonic attraction, or attraction of the same. I call this the Law of Harmonic Attraction. Energy that has a certain wavelength, phase, frequency, will attract energy with exactly the same wavelength, phase and frequency. This Law of Harmonic Attraction creates the phenomena called entrainment.

Entrainment is a type of synchronization. It means that the wavelengths of two different objects come together and take on the same wavelength. To borrow an example from Dr. William Collinge (from Subtle Energy: Awakening to the Unseen Forces in Our Lives), it's like pendulum clocks. In 1665, the inventor of the pendulum clock noticed that, over time, the pendulums in a room full of clocks would all swing together. When he interrupted the pattern, within an hour or two they would all 'sync' back up with each other. All the clocks would entrain with the rate of the one with the biggest pendulum. It put out the strongest wavelength, so the others synchronized to it. They aligned or entrained with the stronger energetic field.

The second type of completion that energy uses is the attraction of the void. This is often explained as 'opposites attract'. I call this the Law of Voidal Attraction. (Apologies if this sounds like jargon. I don't know what else to call it.) This is why electrons with negative charges are attracted to protons with positive charges.

Do you remember that 'Nature abhors a vacuum'? It will send something to fill it up, to complete the picture. Since energy seeks wholeness or completion, it will draw to it that which it needs for completion. It will attract its opposite. This is very often what is at work in intimate relationships.

My first marriage was to Tom Caldwell. Tom was Stability incarnate. I was the epitome of adventure. During our wedding, the ministers who performed the ceremony painted a very appropriate metaphor for Tom and me. They said our relationship was like a tether ball.

Rev. Lark Hapke stood beside Tom and talked about all his attributes. "Tom, you are even-tempered, thoughtful, deliberate, dependable, unwavering, anchored. You, Tom, are the central pole, buried deep in the ground. You are solid, sure, strong. You are the metal bar that rises from the Earth where you are anchored in concrete into the air where you hold the flexible rope that connects you to Phyllis, the tether ball."

Then Rev. Evan Hodkins stood in front of me and talked to our families and friends. "You, Phyllis, are fiery, spontaneous, experimental and experiential, seeking. You are the orb that floats in the air, reaching out beyond the pole, moving in spaces and places the pole doesn't go. It is the cord connecting you to Tom that holds you in bounds, gives you a pattern, a path. It prevents your exploratory nature from spinning you off into outer space. Tom will be your anchor when the storms of life blow through."

Indeed, Tom taught me a lot about how to live a stable life. I had inherited the emotional personality of my alcoholic father who had died of a heart attack when I was 20. Bob Kirk was an intelligent, gregarious, adventurous man who had failed as a father and husband. He was a sporadic provider at best. When I was in fourth grade, I stood alone at the window of our rented house on the poor side of Longmont early one morning. With tears in my eyes, I watched as my mother backed the car out of our driveway on her first day of summer school. It was mother's teaching salary that put food on our table, paid the rent, and got my two sisters and I through college. My dad drove his Lincoln Continental between Longmont and Kansas where he had cattle and sheep.

Tom was everything my dad was not. My dad had a raging temper; Tom never yelled or swore. Dad made and lost fortunes; Tom and I saved and invested the majority of our income. Tom and I lived in a modest town home and drove Mildred and Avery's used Chevrolet Citation. My dad always flaunted his money. When he sold a trainload of cattle and became a millionaire, he bought drinks for the 'whole city of Denver' according to one of dad's friends who was there to participate. My dad was emotionally and physically absent my whole life. But I never had to worry about where Tom was or what he was doing.

Tom was more than a male integrity model for me. I had a relationship Stability void that he filled. He was emotionally and physically present, considerate and supportive. During my twelve years with Tom an additional gift of filling the void was learning financial planning and investing.

Relationships that attract our polar opposites give us the opportunity to learn those qualities that are present in our mates and are missing in us. We are drawn to each other because we fill each others missing parts. And we, like electricity, seek completion.

I had the delight of learning about the 'completion' tradition of one tribe of Native Americans. My teacher was my friend Ward Flynn, author of <u>Truth Zone</u>. His teacher was Basil Braveheart of the Lakota Sioux. The Lakota Sioux see our life journey as an Earthwalk of the Medicine

Wheel. They believe that we are born into one of the four quadrants of the Medicine Wheel: the Warrior, the Healer, the Teacher, or the Spirit Carrier, as I remember it. Where we are born is our power, our trump card. Wisdom comes from using that strength to move into each of the other quadrants, to experience all the facets of life. We are meant to walk in all four quadrants. Look at the Medicine Wheel below.

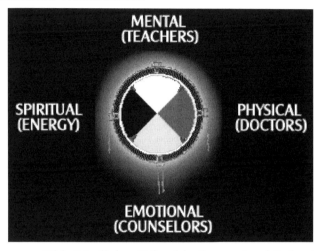

This Medicine Wheel is the work of Robert Kakakaway of the Cree Nation. He does Medicine Wheel training, and I recommend his website at www.kakakaway.com if you are interested in a deeper study of the Medicine Wheel.

Think about which quadrant you feel most comfortable in.

Does this feel like the quadrant you were born into?

Which other quadrants have you walked in?

Which would you like to do next?

Which quadrants are hard for you?

Think of a relationship where you were or are attracted to your opposite.

What quadrant are you in? What quadrant are they in?

How are you opposites?

What are you learning from each other?

What could you learn from each other?

Just as the Sioux sought wisdom in wholeness, so energy seeks completion by both drawing together the same harmonic vibrations and by joining voidal opposites.

So you say, what else is there but same and opposite? Wouldn't that include almost all energy? No, it wouldn't. Harmonic vibrations and voidal opposites are strong, direct, powerful forces. Therefore, it includes all energy that is strong, direct and powerful. The key word here is <u>strongly</u> the same and <u>strongly</u> the opposite.

Everything else is Ho-hum Land. For example, the wavelength 'x' in me for relationships with men is strongly like my father's personality wavelength. I spent the formative years of my life in my father's energetic pool, and that's strong entrainment. So my first husband was the attraction of the opposite of Bob Kirk in the person of Tom Caldwell. As that void of 'male Stability' wavelength was filled, I could later in my life attract relationships with men more like me, more harmonic with my wavelengths. And Tom was able to attract to himself another partner who was much more like him, creating a more fulfilling relationship for him in his second marriage. And the whole range of men between the Bob Kirk model and Tom Caldwell are in Ho-hum Land. They have little attraction for/to me because they are neither strongly like me nor strongly opposite me.

Einstein declared decades ago that everything is energy. The ELM Spectrum shows that only a small fraction (less than 1% per Bucky Fuller) of that energy is visible. As we seek to measure, understand and use the world of non-physical reality, we have to rely on different tools than those we use to measure physical reality. We can begin by relying on our own observations of what is true for us, what works for us, what serves us. See for yourself what is true for you. Look at the synchronicities in your life and begin feeling the patterns that show up.

As we go deeper into the heart of quantum and chaos, that ability to pay attention to what we are attracting to ourselves and why (harmony or the void) is increasingly significant.

Summary – Chapter 1
Einstein and Astrology

I. It's all energy

A. Einstein's proclamation

B. Energy Vibrates

C. Vibrations attract

    1. Strongly alike (entrainment)

    2. Strongly opposite (voidal)

II. Electromagnetic Spectrum - Types of energy

A. Physical

    1. Uses 5 senses

        2. Only 1% of reality

    B. Non-physical

        1. Invisible reality

        2. Must use other tools to perceive it

III. Two laws of Energy Seeking Completion

    A. Attraction of opposites (voidal)

        1. Nature abhors a vacuum

        2. Opposites attract

            a. Phyllis attracted to Tom

            b. Opposite of her father Bob

    B. Attraction of same (harmonic)

        1. Entrainment

        2. Human body's frequencies/waves

            a. Longmont frequency

            b. Scott frequency

            c. Quantum frequency

IV. Heart of quantum and chaos

    A. Non-physical, invisible reality

    B. Requires new tools on the part of the Observer

        1. What is true for me?

        2. What works for me?

        3. What serves me?

    C. Observe my life

1. What patterns come up repeatedly?

2. Look at the synchronicities in my life

D. Pay attention to

1. What do I attract?

2. Why do I attract it?

a. Harmony (attraction of the same)

b. Void (attraction of the opposite)

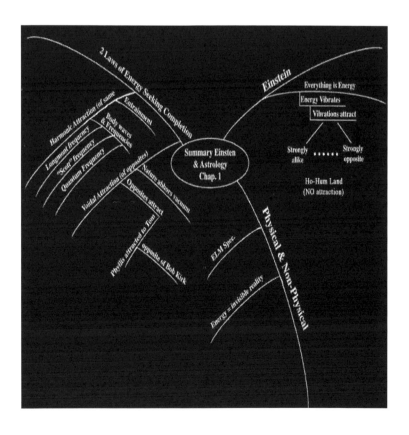

Chapter 2

Systems and the Field

"For my ally is the Force, and a powerful ally it is. Life greets it; makes it grow. Its energy surrounds us and binds us. Luminous beings are we. Not this crude matter. You must feel the Force around you - here, between you, me, the tree, the rock, everywhere.   Yes. Even between the land and the ship."

~ Yoda, "The Empire Strikes Back" Star Wars Trilogy

George Lucas gave Yoda more than just Einstein's face. Yoda has Einstein's wisdom. Yoda is a quantum Jedi. Just as Einstein knew that it's all energy, Yoda knows that that energy encompasses us and relates us to each other. Yoda calls it the Force. Yoda's training as a Jedi master taught him how to become one with the Force. He can use it because he has learned how to operate within its laws - how to use his will and focus to direct the Force. Of course, Darth Vader had the same training. Hence, the dualistic struggle between good and evil, because Darth and Yoda have different intents. In quantum, the Force is called the Field. To understand the field, you must first understand systems.

Seeing Systems

One day my colleague Colleen came into the office and said Scott was warning everyone that the Boulder police were becoming 'parking-meter

Gestapo'. He was upset that a formerly low profile, mild-mannered police force was now 'irrational', 'vigilant', and 'unforgiving' about meter violations. Boulder, Colorado is a town of open space and parks, with a green belt around the city. The foothills have been kept natural with no homes visible from town, and there's a height restriction on commercial buildings. Recently a huge new mall had opened outside Boulder that was a virtual deathblow to Boulder's aging Crossroads Mall. A city revenue bond had just failed.

My neighbor, Beverly Sears, had served on the city council for years. I'd heard her worry about Boulder's decreasing tax base as the council made choice after choice consistent with Boulder's lifestyle, but depleting the city's income that allowed it to offer the quality of living the citizens expected. Her responsibility was the whole of Boulder, and she was able to see the big picture. And here was a classic system's issue. Seeing Boulder as a living system meant not just looking at the 'meter heat' in isolation. Looking at the whole, it was easy to understand that upping the meter violations was a very legitimate way to make up some lost revenue. But you have to learn to think systems.

My first systems teacher was Frank Clement. Frank was the scientist and inventor of the Speakerphone and Touch Screen Computer. He spent nearly three decades with Bell Telephone Systems "in the days when it was the premier R & D organization in the free world." He was proud of the fact that Dr. W. Edwards Deming, the father of Systems Thinking in corporations, had learned about systems from a scientist at Bell Labs. It was, after all, Bell *Systems.*

      Frank was a systems thinker. Despite his intellectual accomplishments, Frank said he wasn't different from anyone else, never called himself a genius. What he had learned, he said, was how to think systemically. Frank taught me the difference between the words 'sys-<u>tem</u>-ic' and 'sys-te-<u>mat</u>-ic.' Systemic deals with the whole, like systemic fertilizer. You can put it on any part of the plant and it will affect the whole plant. Berlitz is a systemic approach to language because it immerses the learner in the whole language. Systematic, on the other hand deals with parts, pieces, step by step processes. Most languages are taught systematically by dissecting the language and teaching it as verbs, grammar, and vocabulary.

      As a systems thinker, Frank went first to the big picture and looked for the inter-relationships. One of Frank's gifts was the ability to simplify and conceptualize difficult material. I'm sure it came from his systems approach to everything. He said it takes ten years to become a systems thinker. While I don't accept that time line, I do know that it takes a conscious effort to begin understanding everything as inter-related systems.

      Have you ever seen a mobile? Below is a system, a model of a mobile.

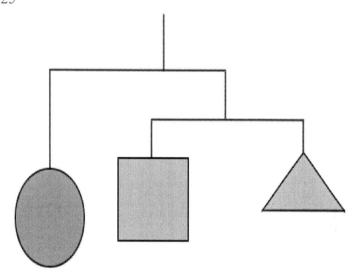

You may have seen the famous mobile by the artist Calder that hangs in the National Gallery of Art. Play with this mobile. Find a spot where you can move one part without moving any other part. What does this tell you about a system?

John Bradford is a family therapist whose programs (The Homecoming, etc.) have been on PBS. He uses the mobile below to represent the family unit. "If Dad's an alcoholic (and he pulls on the dad doll), does it affect the rest of the family? If Muffy's on drugs (and pulls the Muffy figure), is it just Muffy's problem? Is there any individual dysfunction that is not a family problem?" Think about the family mobile below. Could you move one figure without moving the others?

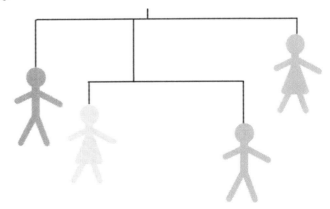

Systems thinking applies to corporations and their subsystems: departments, teams, projects, products, clients, vendors. And systems thinking applies to the individual and to the units within which an individual is a sub-system: families, partnerships, relationships, communities, schools, towns, religions, cultures, nations.

First, it's important to have a feel for what a system is. A system is a combination of things that form a whole that operates in a more complex way than the separate things themselves, like an electrical system or a highway system. It is a coordinated body of objects or processes that have an orderly manner of relating, like the solar system, or a system of government. In a living system, those objects are alive: flexible, growing, changing. Quantum Lite is about the dynamic forces at work in those living systems.

Key Characteristics of Healthy Living Systems

* Balance far from equilibrium

The ability to hold paradox is one of the virtues of the 21st Century Mind, according to Marsha Sinetar in her book Developing a 21st

Century Mind. Balance far from equilibrium is one of those paradoxes. In nature, a system that is close to equilibrium is closest to stagnation (entropy), which is closest to death. So the balance of a thriving system is a flowing balance. Any single direction of activity within the system, seen in isolation, may seem unreliable, unstable or counter-productive. Seen in the perspective of what is happening in the larger system, that activity can be understood as a direction that brings balance to the whole. Jazz and sitar music are examples of balance far from equilibrium.

> "Confusion is uncomfortable, but certainty is ridiculous."
>
> ~ Voltaire

- Multiple feedback loops

A living system is self-referent. It gives itself information on what works and what doesn't work. This information flows through networks of random connections in the system. The system chooses and uses what is beneficial. The information rich feedback of multiple loops is what supports new forms of organization to emerge. They are better adapted to the changing/changed environment. Since nature doesn't have negative judgments which filter or block incoming information, its feedback loops transmit all information.

> "How you see the problem is the problem."
>
> ~ Genevie

- Spontaneous emergence

Spontaneous emergence of order and new forms of behavior happen. As parts come together to form a system, properties emerge that belong only to the whole. These are properties that are not found in the parts. For example: carbon, hydrogen, and oxygen come together and "sweetness" emerges. Sweetness is an emergent property of sugar that cannot be found in any of the smaller components. "The sweetness resides in the relationship," as Fritjof Capra has delightfully elucidated in his book The Web of Life.

Emergence actually has two different forms. There are emergent <u>properties</u> that reside only at higher systems levels, such as the property of sweetness. There are also the mysterious, unpredictable emerging <u>processes</u> that happen in systems far from equilibrium. The observer/participant stands at the edge of chaos remaking itself, waiting to see what will come forth from the turmoil of the old.

> "Problems can become opportunities when the right people come together."
>
> ~ Robert Redford

- Self-making

Systems are self-making, or 'autopoetic'. All changes take place in circular patterns where each change

    - produces other changes

    - maintains the existing pattern, and

    - transforms the existing pattern

> *"The real winners in life are those who look at every situation*

*with an expectation that they can make it
work or make it better."*

~ Barbara Pletcher

- <u>Constant learning</u>

A system learns through constant interaction
with its environment that continuously brings new
information to the system. Every living system is a
learning community. Therefore, a system that is not
constantly learning is dying. Learning happens
through contact of the system with new information
from outside the system. As long as a system is
alive and healthy, it will connect to and link with
input from the environment.

"Where all think alike, no one thinks very
much."

~ Walter Lippmann

- <u>Knowing (cognizant)</u>

the ability to generate information

the capacity to receive feedback

the power to self-regulate

A living system is cognizant, knowing. It is
aware of its environment. A living system has the
ability to deal with information in a way that
generates order and self-organization. Such a
system knows what its purpose is. It makes itself
based on the memory of its pattern even as various
internal segments die, change or regenerate. The
memories of the organism remain and are the
known pattern around which the new segments
form.

"I want to know what sustains you from the
inside when all else falls away."

~ Oriah Mountain Dreamer

- Closed for functions; Open for information

The system is closed in that a specific process happens and specific patterns are maintained inside the boundaries of the system. The system exists for a specific purpose, to perform a function. The boundaries themselves, however, are leaky, spongy, and open. The system draws information and energy from the environment surrounding it through its porous boundaries.

In a healthy self-organizing system, boundaries are not fixed or permanent. They are a fluid net that allows the organism to define what is inside and what is outside. There is a constant flow through these boundaries. They are not walls of exclusion, but webs that facilitate the movement of information in and out.

When a fluorescent dye is dropped into a single cell in a cluster of healthy cells, where the healthy cells share a boundary with a cluster of cancer cells, the dye (information) will travel quickly through all the healthy cells. Little, if any, dye will cross into the cancer cells. When the dye is dropped into the middle of the cancer cells, it does not spread. The walls of a healthy cell are a means of transporting information. But the walls of cancer cells are boundaries that block it.

"The best leaders are very often

the best listeners.

They have an open mind. They are not
interested in having their own way,

but in finding the best way."

~Wilfred Peterson

Self-organizing Systems and Sub-systems

All of these characteristics create living,
self-organizing systems. It was from my next
systems teachers that I learned about self-
organizing. Those teachers were Dr. Margaret
(Meg) Wheatley and Dr. Fritjof Capra.

Frank and I met Meg Wheatley and Fritjof
Capra at her conference "Self-Organizing Systems:
A Simpler Way" in Sundance, Utah. Meg was the
first person to apply quantum thinking to the
corporate world. I believe that time will prove
Meg's first book Leadership and the New Science to
be a pivotal contribution in unifying the centuries
old split between science and spirit as well as
unifying the worlds of science, spirit and business.
An easier read is her sequel A Simper Way, written
with Myron Kellner-Rogers.

Fritjof Capra is an Austrian-born theoretical
physicist turned writer. (The Tao of Physics,
Turning Point, Belonging to the Universe, and The
Science of Life: Integrating the Hidden Connections
Among the Biological, Cognitive and Social
Dimensions of Life.) His Web of Life is a brilliant
explanation of the significance of interrelated self-
organizing systems in nature. Fritjof also wrote the
screenplay for "Mindwalk." For those couch
potatoes who don't want to read, go to Amazon and

order the video "Mindwalk." It's filmed at the
island-abbey Mont St. Michel, and stars Liv
Ullmann, Sam Waterston, and John Heard. It's the
CliffsNotes for Quantum Physics 101 in story form,
an enjoyable video set in the breath taking beauty of
coastal France. It will help you understand what
Fritjof means when he says that 'understanding the
pattern of self organization is the key to
understanding the essential nature of life.'

It was at Meg's workshop in Sundance, Utah
that my soul caught fire. In the company of Meg
and Fritjof and learning about Dr. Prigogine's work,
I felt a passion ignite in me for the quantum world. I
saw its possibilities for we ordinary non-scientists.
It was a peak experience where the pieces fell into
place. The following week, I designed what I
humbly called the Kirk Model of Chaos. Frank
liked it, and we put it into a new workshop on self-
organizing systems called Quantum Leadership. I
was delighted and awed to see how quickly people
got the model and how profound their resulting
insights were. I eventually had the opportunity to
show the Kirk Model to Dr. Prigogine personally,
and get his blessing and encouragement - another
peak life experience.

All this time I was learning more about
living systems. All living systems are self-
organizing. Self-organizing means exactly what it
says: a system has the ability to organize itself.

Self-organizing happens in both the world of
corporations and the private lives of individuals.
Said another way, it happens at both the macro and
micro level of systems. The macro is the bird's eye
view of the organization. It starts with a large
system and refines inward to the sub-systems. The

micro, or individual view, is the reverse. It starts from the view of an individual human and expands outward through all the larger systems in which that human participates. Here are two fictional models for these concepts under the assumed names of ORB, Inc., for the organization and Rose Oliver as the personal system. Orb will be used to show how systems look in organizations, and Rose's life will show how systems work with individuals.

Rose Oliver is a total system that has many sub-systems. * She is an employee, supervisor, mother, daughter, spouse, sister, homemaker, citizen, church member, singer, and friend. She can't separate out "employee" and not have it affected by "mother" as every working parent knows. Every sub-system acts on and reacts to every other sub-system that makes up her total system. In turn, Rose Oliver is a sub-system in ORB, Inc. where she works.

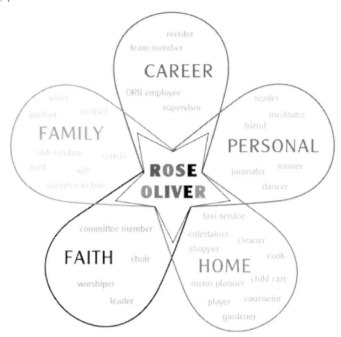

* I struggle with the word 'sub-system', especially when talking about human beings. It seems antiseptic, cold, and scientific. One quantum physicist (Gregory Bateson, I believe) coined the word 'whole-ons' for us as humans in the larger Earth system. Whole-on seems robotic and little better that sub-system. Until someone finds a better word, I'll use sub-system. If you aren't a purist and want a simpler word for sub-system, you can say 'part.' Just don't say it in front of Meg Wheatley.

In the same way as Rose, ORB as a system cannot separate its sub-systems and have an effective whole. What happens if R & D doesn't communicate with Production; if Finance doesn't talk to Marketing; if HR isn't working with Finance? The success of ORB relies on healthy relationships between departments. Remember the dye and the healthy cells? Lots of communication. What was the symptom of the cancer cells? Little transfer of information; no interactive relationship with the units around it. As Meg Wheatley says, "Information is the lifeblood of an organization."

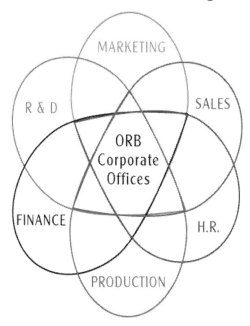

Quantum and chaos and the Kirk Model (which you will see in Chapter 3) operate in big systems and little systems. Look back at the diagrams of ORB, Inc. and Rose Oliver. Which roles can you eliminate without affecting the whole? When a variety of functions or pieces come together and become a system, they are no longer 'parts', according to Meg Wheatley. 'Parts' means you can disassemble the unit and have the original separate pieces. You can't do this with a system because a system is a synergistic whole. The accepted definition of synergistic is 'the whole is greater than its parts'. However, Bucky Fuller, who coined the word 'synergy', says, "Synergy means the behavior of the whole cannot be predicted from the behavior of the parts".

You as a System

You are now going to experience yourself as a system.

The name of my system is Phyllis Ruth Kirk. What is the name of your system?

What is the purpose of your system? (If you want the easy answer, here's a hint: My system's purpose is to be Phyllis-ing.)

Describe what your system looks like to others.

What are the sub-systems within your system? (Your muscles are your muscular system, your blood is your circulatory system, your bones are your skeletal system, etc.)

Which system(s) can you leave out?

What parts of any system can you leave out? (Appendix? Gall bladder?)

What happens to the system when a part is taken out?

Now think of yourself as a sub-system in a larger system. This one is fun. Think of all the larger systems that you are a sub-system in: (I am a sister in the system of my birth family; I am a mother in the system of my marital family; I am a friend in the system of my life relationships; I am a contributor in the www.EmptyHandsMusic.com system, in the www.TheOptimist.com system, etc)

Consciousness

By definition, all living systems are self-organizing systems. A system knows its purpose and continues to do its purpose if left uninterrupted. This is a form of consciousness. The system knows why it exists.

This knowing is a key ingredient in self-organizing living systems. As such, it is also a critical element in chaos as will be explained later. For now, it's important to understand how consciousness creates the field of the system.

The central purpose of a system is its core vibration. It's like the DNA of a system. It's what the system is coded to do, to be. ORB's consciousness comes from it mission statement, its goals, it values, its unique product. There literally is an energy field, a non-physical energetic vibration, that is ORB. You can feel that field when you walk through the doors of any organization: Is this organization vibrant, healthy? Do the people who work here like working here? Is there a sense of pride in what this company produces? Do the employees like coming to work on Monday mornings? Is the company's central purpose clear to every person who works there? Do they know why they are there?

Rose Oliver's central purpose is to be the best Rose Oliver she can be. Her goal is to discover what is unique about herself, why she is here, what it is that she can do/be/contribute that only Rose can do. Her purpose is to be "Rose-ing". That means growing, choosing, taking actions in alignment with her unique self.

Knowing our purpose is critical. It is critical to our happiness. And it is critical to every system we are in. Every one of us benefits deeply by knowing what our uniqueness is. Martin Sage, head of Sage Productions, is especially gifted at helping people do this. He asks, "What are you the Picasso of? What is your passion? What lights your fire?" Joseph Campbell, anthropologist and author of The Masks of God, says, "Find your bliss. Find where it is and don't be afraid to follow it."

In Boulder, Colorado, New Vista is a public magnet high school. Its two goals for each and every student are:

#1: Help that person discover their uniqueness;

#2: Help them develop and enhance it in a productive, responsible direction.

At a New Vista graduation, master teacher John Zola quoted Sidney Smith. "By the time a person reaches 16, they should be able to stand with their peers, their family, and those they love, and talk for fifteen minutes on 'What the world would be missing if I were not here.' " Think how beautiful the world would be if every person knew what their special gifts are and knew how to contribute to the health of the whole by using those talents.

Your uniqueness is important to all the systems you are a part of. A system is strengthened by diversity. The more diverse a system is, the more options it has. The more homogenous it is, the weaker it is. It has a narrower range of responses, fewer choices when challenged, and less material to create with. 'Strength in diversity' isn't just a corporate HR ploy. It is a truth in nature. That's why biodiversity strengthens a system. When you contribute your uniqueness to a system, you strengthen that system.

A system, whether it's ORB, Inc. or Rose Oliver, is stronger during chaos if it knows who it is . . . and isn't. When a system becomes unsettled or disturbed, one of the first things it does is to look for handholds-things to hold onto while the boat rocks. To the degree that the system is clear about its purpose, it will connect with handholds that serve it in the long run. To the degree that a system does not know its purpose, it will reach for and take hold of the closest, easiest thing to grasp. Those things can be a disservice to it in the long run, when chaos really shakes things up.

That consciousness of purpose is a field of energy. Every living system has a field. It is a non-physical zone of vibrations that emanate from the system. As a human being or a corporation, the strength of clarity and commitment you have to your purpose determines the strength of your system's field. When it's strong in a person, it's called charisma. It's magnetic. It attracts to you others who have similar interests, literally, similar vibrations.

One of the first classes in Chaos 101 is 'Who Am I?' As a system, an individual human or corporation you need to know: Who are you? How are you unique? What are your goals? What is your purpose in life? Do your actions prove it?

The clearer you are about who you are as a system, the stronger will be your ability to self-organize during times of instability. You will attract to you the support you need to maintain your functions. Clarity of purpose is like your body's immune system. When your immune system is strong, you do not succumb to the germs that are in the air all the time. When you are stressed, worried, not eating right, overworked, lacking balance and play in your life, your body gets weak. When your immune system is weak is when germs and viruses can take hold and make you sick.

Louis Pasteur discovered the microbe, or 'germ' as we have nicknamed it. On his deathbed, he said, "I have been greatly misunderstood. The germ is nothing. The environment is everything." The environment of the germ is the body's condition. Pasteur knew that it is not germs that make us sick, but a weak immune system.

Just so, when your larger system's clarity of purpose is strong, you have a better chance of staying on track during chaos and disorder.

Cycles of Life

All living systems have cycles. As the Bible says, "For everything there is a season. A time to sew, a time reap . . ."

Life is meant to ebb and flow, to grow larger, then smaller. A balanced human being goes out actively into the world and then returns home for rest, nurturing and recharging. Ideally, organizations should allow, nay, promote, the same thing for the organization: production and growth followed by a period of rest and renewal.

During my years in Moscow, my Soviet friends were always eager to point out the superiority of their socialist vacations. Every worker got 6 to 8 weeks' annual vacation. They would say, "Your capitalistic treadmill is killing your people. Look at the high level of stress-related diseases you have." Indeed, it is ludicrous to think that two weeks of rest can neutralize fifty weeks of work stress. We are deceiving ourselves to believe that setting aside 14 days of relaxation will renew, balance and recharge us for the remaining 351 days. This balance of work and rest may be rejected by Wall Street's growth mentality, but it is the natural pattern of living systems.

Order and chaos are another cycle in the natural pattern. A living self-organizing system in chaos, left alone, will move to a state of order. Order is when there's a place for everything, and everything is in its place. It is 'a condition in which each thing is properly disposed with reference to other things and to its purpose.' For ORB, it means the organizational chart, the goals and the short, medium, and long term strategies are in place (Who we are; What we do; How we get there). For Rose Oliver, order means she has a job description and a workspace, the competence and equipment to do her job, access to and support from the personnel and processes she needs, free flow of information, and a clear understanding why her job is important to ORB's success.

A healthy living system, left alone to follow its own natural rhythm, will grow into a state of disorder and chaos. Chaos (as if it needs any description.) is a state of utter confusion, turmoil, uncertainty. Even the words can make our stomach knot, our breath shallow, our fists clench. Chaos at ORB means in-fighting between departments, power struggles blocking the flow of information, a flood of new employees overwhelming HR, new competitors grabbing your share of the market, a new CEO changing goals in mid-project, computer systems breaking down . . . and no product being made. For Rose, chaos is all of the above because she's a sub-system in the ORB mess. And for her own sub-system, it also means her baby getting sick, her husband being laid off, an aging parent, having a car accident, a fire in the house, her pet dying.

Chaos is when all the handholds are gone and the earth is rolling under our feet. Whatever our former security was, it isn't there now. We feel alone, abandoned, terrified. It is the time and place that St. John of the Cross called 'the dark night of the soul'.

You cannot avoid chaos if you are a healthy living system. You can only go through it. For ORB, no amount of strategic planning, inventories or 401(k)'s will eliminate chaos. For Rose, no amount of wealth, degrees or insurance policies will prevent it. It is part of life and it will happen.

Nature doesn't mind chaos. Humans do. Chaos is uncomfortable because we aren't in charge. We can't control chaos, by definition, so we don't like it. But nature doesn't worry about control. It doesn't try to squelch a hurricane, or stop an earthquake. The reason (and one of my favorite Frank Clement quotes) is:

"Molecules don't have an attitude."

It is we mere humans who try to interfere with natural cycles. Our deeply engrained socialization has convinced us that order is good and disorder is bad. But nature experiences that a hurricane shakes the deadwood out of the trees and the forest grows back stronger because of it. A forest fire replenishes the soil and earthquakes spew mineral rich stuff all over the ground. But for humans in the midst of the destruction, it's hard to

remember that nature uses chaos constructively. As
Eric Lyleson says,

>Creativity happens when we are dancing

>on the edge of chaos.

So the question then becomes, if we can't
control chaos or avoid it, what do we do during
chaos? Give up and be swept into the cyclone of
change, desperately hoping the results might be
beneficial to us? Surrender and let our lives bob
around aimlessly on the 'natural' tumultuous seas?

The human being is both an element of
nature and a force within nature. We cannot
eliminate or manage chaos. Our challenge is to
learn to trust the process and our own power to
create. Our responsibility is to participate and,
through chaos, to create. Learning how to do that is
what Quantum Lite is about.

>"Understanding chaos makes us want to
>participate in creation."

>~ Dr. Ilya Prigogine

The Field

Every living system has an electromagnetic
(ELM) field of energy around it. It is non-physical
(invisible), but measurable in many cases. That field
is both magnetic and projective. In science, we
learned one of Newton's laws, "that every living
thing attracts every other living thing". The field
acts as an attractor to draw information and energy
to it that the system needs from the surrounding
environment. That's the 'charisma' of the system, so
to speak. At the same time it puts information about

itself out into the surroundings. That's the broadcast capacity of the system. That energetic projection/magnetism is what Yoda was teaching Luke Skywalker in his first lesson about the Force.

When you walk into a home, an office, a shop, a party, you get an intuitive hit about the environment. It may be as basic as, "This feels great. I like this place", or "OOOOOOOOO this feels bad! Get me outta here!" (Remember the pop song 'Momma Told Me Not to Come'?) You are tuning into the field, the overall effect of the combined energies of that place, and how they affect your field.

As you learn to read the field and your intuition better, the same thing works with individuals. You can walk into a group of strangers and know immediately. You are drawn to some of them, interested in getting to know them. Others you are neutral about, disinterested. Some you may want to actively avoid. This information may come partly from body language or outward appearances. But a blind person gets all this information without the benefit of sight. The sighted have simply not developed the ability to read the non-physical information of the field, nor the trust to rely on it. One challenge of living the quantum life is to learn to read the non-physical as clearly as the non-sighted read it.

Summary - Chapter 2
Systems and the Field

I. What Are Systems

A. Definition of system: A combination of things that form a whole that operates in a more complex way than the separate things themselves.

B. Everything is systems of energy

II. Systems Thinkers/Systems Thinking

A. Frank Clement

B. Meg Wheatley, Fritjof Capra

C. Dr. Ilya Prigogine

III. Systems and Sub-systems

A. Human as a system made up of sub-systems (Rose Oliver)

B. Human as a sub-system within larger systems (Rose within ORB)

C. Corporation as a system with sub-systems (ORB)

IV. Living Systems

A. Characteristics

    1. Balance far from equilibrium

    2. Multiple feedback loops

    3. Self-making

    4. Constant learning

5. Knowing (cognizant)

6. Closed for functions; Open for information

B. All living systems are self-organizing systems

C. Consciousness of purpose is the critical organizing force in systems

V. Living Systems Have Natural Cycles

A. Growth and rest cycle

B. Chaos. . . order. . . chaos. . . order cycle

C. Definition of chaos; of order

D. All living systems experience chaos

1. Nature: "Molecules don't have an attitude."

2. Humans: resist chaos because we believe it will hurt us; can't control it.

E. Human responsibility is to create through participation during chaos

VI. Consciousness

A. Living systems in nature know their purpose

B. Central purpose is core vibration similar to the system's DNA

C. Knowing our purpose is vital when chaos comes (for both humans and corporations)

D. The larger system is healthy when each sub-system knows its purpose.

VII. The Field

A. ELM energy surrounding every system

B. Yoda calls it the Force

C. Purpose of the Field during chaos is to draw to the system the things it needs to survive, reform itself

D. Relied on by the non-sighted

E. Learn to read the Field

Chapter 3

Chaos

Chaos in Nature

I am on a writing sabbatical on the southeastern Caribbean island of St. Vincent. It is the beginning of November which is the end of hurricane season. My cottage has a view of the ocean on an isolated part of the island. There are only four houses in view and six neighbors: 2 Vincentians, a Jamaican, a Canadian and 2 ex-pat gringos. They've all lived through hurricanes. I haven't.

There is a storm raging. As the wind and rain increase in intensity, they tell me that St. Vincent is in the path of hurricane Lenny. I have no TV so they are my weather forecasters and news reporters. This hurricane, they say, is not following the only known pattern of hurricanes: coming from the southeast. It is the first hurricane ever to begin inside the Gulf of Mexico to the west and move eastward. And I got to experience it.

The government of SVG (St. Vincent and the Grenadines) had just completed a beautiful new tourist dock and harbor shopping complex. It had not yet been dedicated when Lenny struck with wave action in the opposite direction of what it was built for. It was destroyed before it saw its first cruise ship.

"Human memory goeth not to the contrary" is a phrase used by Dean Angus McSwain in my Property I class at Baylor Law School. It means we can't remember a time when it wasn't like it is now. Until Lenny. It seems we are now living in times of unprecedented unpredictability everywhere . . . and therefore (according to quantum thought) unprecedented potential.

I'd had an Aha! at the Sundance conference. It was an insight on how chaos can work for us. It was triggered by Dr. Prigogine's work on unpredictability and non-linearity. In 1977 Dr. Prigogine turned classical thermodynamics on its ear with his Theory of Dissipative Structures. The Second Law of Thermodynamics basically says that heat only goes spontaneously from an object of hotter temperature to an object of colder temperature. In a simple gloomy metaphor, it says the earth is like a mechanical clock that has been wound up. It is slowly winding down, stagnating and dying . . . headed for 'heat death'. Dr. Prigogine said: Not necessarily so. He proved, and received the Nobel Prize for showing, that some systems can, in fact, develop in an upward spiral of ever-increasing complexity.

He put a Bunsen burner under a beaker of clear liquid and added new chemicals. When confronted with enormous rapid change, the system fell apart as predicted. But then, instead of dying, this 'chemical clock' spontaneously turned from blue to red to clear again as millions of molecules instantaneously rearranged themselves. Yes, the chaos had blown the system apart. But instead of disintegrating, the system came together at a higher level of complexity.

Thanks to Dr. Prigogine's work, we can now see chaos as a catalyst that allows us to fall apart so that we can come back together at a higher level. That transformed system is now more complex, more diverse and more resilient than the old system.

Theory of Dissipative Structures and

Kirk Chaos Model

Prigogine's Theory of Dissipative Structures (greatly simplified) goes like this. A living system gets new information (Energy Rich Input or ERI) from its surroundings. The new information upsets the system because it doesn't have any place to put this previously unknown 'stuff'. This stress on the system causes waves of agitation ('perturbation' in Prigogine's words). The agitated waves run into themselves (feedback), increasing the shakeup until the system is frantic.

During the chaos, a human system can react either as a system that values *Stability* (an 'S' system) or as a system that values *Balance* (a 'B' system). A Balance-seeking or B system has high energy exchange: lots of information and energy flowing in, around and out. A Stability-seeking or S system has a low energy exchange. It gets a lot of ERI and holds onto it, creating a blockage or energy build-up.

When the chaotic energy has stretched the system to its max, it reaches its Tolerance Boundary - the point beyond which the system cannot stretch. (We've all been there.) And the system explodes. Prigogine calls this the 'bifurcation point'. 'Bi' means 'two' as in bicycle with two wheels; and 'furcation' means 'fork'. The explosion brings the system to a fork in the road and it can go one of two ways.

The system will break apart, disintegrate and die. Or, it will 'snap' instantly to a new, higher level of structure now able to handle more ERI.

Below is the Kirk Model of Chaos applying Prigogine's Theory of Dissipative Structures to social systems. Dr. Prigogine says, "As humans, we are the best expressions of natural laws." This model applies his revolutionary scientific theory to human systems: individuals, families, corporations, nations. It has meaning for us personally, professionally, and organizationally. This first example is for a corporate system.

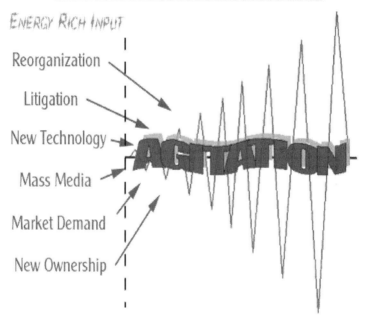

Figure 1

Kirk Model of Chaos (KMC)

The first part of the chaos cycle.

Figure 1 shows the first part of the chaos cycle. The existing system receives Energy Rich Input (ERI) from the environment outside the system. For a corporation, this can be: expansion of markets; technological improvements; change in regulation/legislation; competitor's new strategy; global political events; litigation; merger/acquisition; etc. The energy rich input does not find places waiting to receive it. It's an uninvited guest crashing the party. It doesn't fit into the existing structure of the system. Its entrance into the system with no place to go puts the system into agitation, or 'perturbation'. The agitation is gentle at first, but the effect of feedback loops feeding back in on themselves continues to increase the disturbance of the existing system.

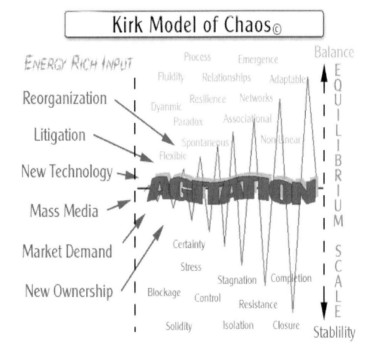

Figure 2

Kirk Model of Chaos (KMC), second part.

Reactions to agitation caused by the ERI.

Figure 2 shows the different ways that a living system can react to the agitation caused by the ERI. The right vertical dotted line shows the range of movement within the living system. It's the scale of Balance or Stability called the Equilibrium Scale.

Look at the bottom ½ of the figure, below the word AGITATION. It shows a system which is closest to *Stability*. It has minimum movement. It is close to stagnation (entropy), which is closest to death. It does not have a lot of energy flowing through it, similar to a cold cup of coffee. These systems are: stagnant, clogged, suspended, moldy, monotonous, rigid, etc.

Now look at the top half of the figure. It shows a system that is in, or seeking, Balance. It is at the other end of the movement scale. It has lots of energy moving around in it. A system seeking Balance is: agile, active, flexible, energetic, responsive, adapting, etc.

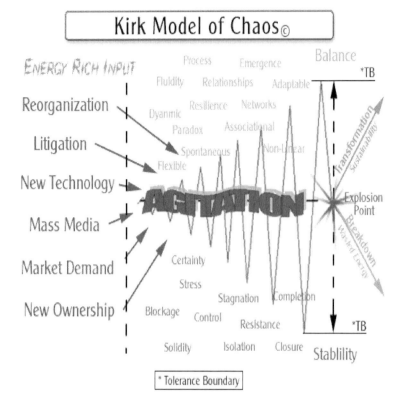

Figure 3 - Kirk Model of Chaos (KMC)

The system at explosion point.

Figure 3 shows the end of the chaos cycle. At the height of agitation, the frantic energy is banging against the Tolerance Boundaries. The system cannot hold any more shakeup, and it explodes. This is the bifurcation point. This explosion allows the system to go in one of two directions. One, the system experiences a breakdown or dis-integration where the fiber of the former structure shatters and the pieces blow out and fall in a heap. Or, two, the system experiences a snap, an instant transformation to a higher, more complex structure. This new form is now able to handle the increased ERI.

The First Law of Thermodynamics says that energy is neither created nor destroyed. It is only converted or transformed. So energy is not destroyed in either breakdown or transformation. It is 'dissipated' as in Theory of Dissipative Structures. When the system breaks down, energy is released and scattered. This energy is wasted because it does not directly produce growth. It doesn't contribute to a higher living form. But the energy, which is scattered during transformation, comes back together at a higher level and does directly contribute to the growth of the system. In the case of transformation, the energy is most efficiently used to grow the system. In the case of breakdown, there is wasted energy.

Just as with the ELM Spectrum, the energy in the system has two forms: one form is the physical, solid, visible stuff - the material elements. The other form is the non-physical, invisible, energetic substance - the pattern. The pattern is the memory blueprint. It is an energetic web or matrix. Think of it as an invisible vibrating spider web giving off a frequency that signals the explosion-scattered elements. Those elements that are vibrating at the same frequency will be drawn to the newly forming system. Those that aren't will drift and fall.

A corporate example of this is a railroad company in the 1950's. We'll call it Land R&R. Their system has been thrown into chaos by the ERI of airplanes as commercial carriers not just military hardware. Land R&R becomes frantic as competition increases, clients desert them and revenues fall. Those elements (people) stuck in Stability mentality are in denial, "Don't worry. Planes are too dangerous, too expensive. People will never use them." Those who accept the inevitable competition are saying, "Buy more land. Lay more track. Build bigger trains."

But somewhere in BalanceLand, someone is thinking systemically, rising above the maddening crowd and looking at the big picture. They get an 'Aha!' "Might it be that we're not in the railroad business? Might it be that we're in the *transportation* business!" As the railroad company goes bankrupt (explosion point), two things happen. There were those who only knew, thought or invested their energy in railroads. They will disintegrate and fall in a heap among other bitter, angry, resentful 'victims' of the growing air industry. But those who are excited about being in the transportation business will be getting together. A new company, AirTrack is born. It is full of the former employees of Land R&R who are adaptive, lateral thinkers, big picture people. They succeed because their goal is to give great transportation service and they have experience in service. They have self-selected from among the shattering pieces because of their sympathetic vibrations. They come together "because they know they belong together."

This insight is from Albie Merrill, a friend and colleague at Boeing. I had asked, 'But WHY do these pieces come together again at a higher level after explosion?" Albie simply said, "Because they know they belong together." Her answer triggered my ruminations on how it looks energetically when things "know they belong together".

The History of the Organism

So, the next obvious question is, "How can we get transformation instead of collapse?" Fritjof Capra's answer to that question is the heart of the significance of the chaos model. Nature doesn't give guarantees. But, according to Fritjof, "the *history* of the organism (system) tends to be determinative at the bifurcation point."

What does the history of a system look like? Can we consciously choose that history in ways that will favor growth not death? Can we hedge our bets? If so, how?

To answer these questions, I relied on the Bucky Fuller approach of using myself as the guinea pig. Since I am a living system, what did my history look like? My history began at eighteen when I started making my own significant life choices. I like the image of altars that mark the significant events in our lives. My friend Rev. Lark Hapke gave this metaphor to me. She was talking about Sarah and Abraham wandering in the desert with the Israelites. Wherever they stopped and spent a part of their lives, they would build an altar. Through the decades, they could look back on where they'd been, figuratively speaking, by looking back at the places they'd built altars in the desert.

As I looked at the altars of my own history, I realized that the external actions were only the results. The real history was what was happening inside me that made me make the choices I made. I then began looking at my emotional development as my history. What were the psychological motivators for each action I'd taken?

Look back at KMC #3. Look at the space between the uprights of the goal posts. (For the sports-challenged, that's the two dotted vertical lines.) This space is the 'cooking time.' The cooking time begins when the ERI enters the system and ends at explosion. An orderly, good-running system is like a pan of cold water sitting on a stove. The entry of ERI information is like turning the burner on under the pan. The water goes from cold to cool to warm to hot. Bubbles appear on the bottom. Then they turn loose of the bottom, float to the top and break the surface, causing a ripple. The size and speed of the bubbles builds, increasing the turmoil in the water. When it reaches a rolling boil, the explosion point comes. One of two things happens at this bifurcation point. (1) Your pot boils over (if you cook like I do) spilling out of the system; or (2) the water evaporates, "dissipates" to use Prigogine's word. The boiled-over water represents the lost or wasted energy. The steam represents the transformation. The water has turned into a gas which is now able to handle more ERI, or heat.

The cooking time is critical in the chaos process. It is the history of the system. It is the time period where our decisions make the patterns that can decide the outcome at the explosion point. It is the blueprint that will sustain itself or vanish after the explosion. If the patterns are clear and strong then the memory of the pattern will magnetize the scattered elements back to each other. They will regroup in ways that are better suited to the new conditions. What results is stronger for the new environment. Voila! A sustainable system.

Since Fritjof says the history of the organism tends to be the determining factor whether I transform or breakdown, I looked at the places where I had crashed and burned. (An interesting note is that it was much easier for me to identify the burnouts than the transformations.) Those breakdowns were: after five years as a lawyer at the Solicitor's Office; after three years in Moscow; after Frank's illness and death; after eight years at BCAL; after five months at Arroyo Beach Resort (living in AC in a gated, manicured community instead of my open air jungle home). What were the unhealthy choices I'd made 'during the cooking time' that ended my chaos in burnout in each case? What I saw was a pattern of specific personal behaviors that determined I was headed for breakdown:

- an on-going need for excitement and adventure (constant action and diversion);

- a need to be seen as unique, special (self-centered, attention-seeking);

- a need to do things differently, be a pioneer (lots of struggle);

- an attitude of total self-reliance, "I'll do it myself, thank you." (extreme independence and self-sufficiency)

- the inability to ask for help, to admit I was in over my head, to tell myself I didn't know what I was doing (driven to appear competent)

- cutting myself off from friends, family; not asking for input from those who knew and loved me; resistance to hearing input (isolation);

- fear of embarrassment and/or public humiliation (pride and vanity);

- fear of disappointing people who (I thought) wanted me to be something I wasn't (pretending, pleasing);

- afraid to leave the familiar even though it was hurting me because I didn't know what else to do, where to go, how to earn money (controlled by a need for financial security);

- being in selfless service; giving 90% of my personal energy away to another person, cause or organization (rescuing; co-dependency; lack of life Balance)

Here's the chaos model showing my history. It's a summary of the patterns in my system's history that have caused me breakdown. This shows the Chaos Model for a personal system, as opposed to the ones above that are for a corporate system. (Patterns that tend to cause transformation come in later chapters. We'll take the bitter pill first, and have dessert later.)

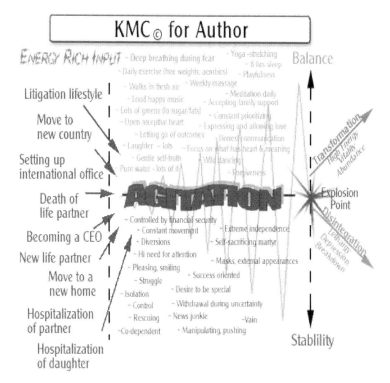

Figure 5

KMC as a personal chaos model

Now look at your own history, either personally or organizationally. Where are the places you had burnout or breakdown? What were the behaviors that led to it?

When did you have transformations? What were you doing during the time of agitation, the 'cooking time' that contributed to your transformation?

Look at the patterns you held onto from the time the new information first hit you until the explosion point. Those patterns are the history that can determine whether your breakdown or transform after you explode. Every system will explode. It means the system is changing, reaching for the opportunity to grow. But every system will not disintegrate. The system can transform if the patterns are strong enough to draw it together again.

A pattern is a repeated behavior. Ask yourself, "What things do I do consistently when my environment is shakey?" Especially, "What are my patterns when I am stressed?" The bottom line is, when you get stressed, do you reach for Stability or can you 'hang loose' and seek Balance?

Reaching for Stability during chaos looks like this. "Why can't we just keep things the way they were?" "I KNOW what is RIGHT!" "I'm the boss, do it my way." "Follow the rules." ""I want to get this done, NOW!" "Don't ask questions." "Move over. I'll do it." "I don't see any problem." "I'm fine. Leave me alone." "It's your fault. You should have. . . " "Ignore it. It'll go away." "It's hopeless. I'm doomed."

The more you insist on Stability, the more rigid your system is. A rigid system shatters at explosion. Think of a glass Christmas ornament. What happens when you hit it with a bat (new energy rich information coming into the system fast)?

On the other hand, seeking Balance during chaos looks like this. "Uh-oh, something's happening here." "Hey, maybe this is different than last time." "So, what do you think?" "Are there other solutions I haven't thought of?" "Why do you think this is happening?" "What am I doing that works? What am I doing that doesn't work?" "Who do I know that I can ask to help me with this?" "I know life will look better tomorrow." "Am I breathing, staying calm, paying attention to what really matters to me?" "Am I open to the possibilities that can come out of this?" "Do I accept that I may need to do some changing?" "What could be the message in this situation for me?" "What can I learn from this?" "Can I accept that action, even if I don't agree with it?" And, of course, the ultimate and rarely- seen response to chaos, "Wow! What an opportunity!"

The more you allow the flow of events to move through you or by you without getting hooked into the emotions and holding onto the dramas, the more flexible you stay. Forgiveness. Adaptability. Acceptance. Openness. Receptivity. Staying present. Responsiveness. Valuing relationship more than being right. Breathing. All are important if you want to maintain your Balance during chaos. But remember, it is a Balance far from equilibrium. There will be moments (hours? days? weeks?) when you do not feel in Balance. In the long run, your system is in Balance. The more flexible you stay, the faster your system can respond. Think of the rigid glass ball and the bat. Now think of a willow branch. What happens when you hit it with a baseball bat? It's the same energy rich information coming into a system at the same speed. Does the willow branch shatter? Why not?

Below is your own personal chaos model. Think of a time when you were in rapid change. Print out the KMC and fill it in. What was the new information (Energy Rich Input) that came into your system? What did the agitation look like? What were your responses that were Stability seeking? What were your responses that were Balance seeking?

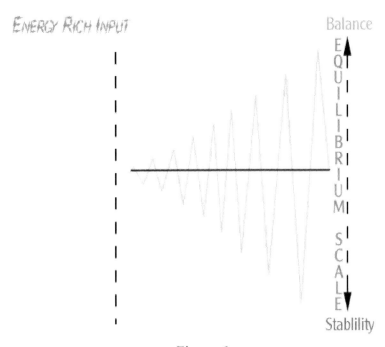

Figure 6
My Personal Chaos Model

After you've filled in your Chaos Model, take your journal and write about these questions. As you're doing it, remember, nature doesn't do Good/Bad, Right/Wrong. Try simply being a silent witness to your actions without judging them. Look at them as if you are watching a play about someone else's life, and ask, "What could s/he learn from this scenario? What could s/he do different that might give a different result?" (You are allowed to say ugly things about the star of the show only if you're laughing while doing it.) When you're really proud of yourself, you get to give yourself the Academy Award for Best Screenplay.

What did you feel like when your system reached its Tolerance Boundary (total chaos, just before explosion)?

What did the Explosion Point feel like?

What were the two paths you could have taken at the bifurcation (Explosion Point)? Did you disintegrate or transform?

What patterns did you form during the cooking time that could have determined that result?

"The difference between a comedy

and a tragedy is that

in a comedy the characters figure out reality

in time to do something about it".

-- Bennett W. Goodspeed

Misfits in the System

Remember the fate of Land R&R? Look at Figure 4 above. What if you are an S (Stability-seeking person) and you are in a B (Balance-seeking) system? For example, you are a fifty-year-old WASP, you like tradition, consistency, rules, regular hours, clear job description. Your company has just been bought by ZippyCo. ZippyCo's President and CEO is twenty-five years old. She (oh, yes) declares flex time, everyone's their own boss, the team determines pay and promotions, all projects are group efforts, etc. What may happen to you?

Or suppose you are a B in an S family? Your dad has worked in the same factory for 25 years and your mother is a homemaker. They were both born in the same small mid-western town you are growing up in. Your older brother and sister both got married after high school, and are now raising their families in your small town. All social life centers around the church and town you grew up in. At age twelve, you announced you were vegetarian, you love theater and dance, and your dream is to study in New York. What will happen to you when the family goes into crisis about your choice to leave home after high school?

There's a great thing about being different from the sub-system you are in. At the explosion, you get to join a group of people who are like-spirited. An S will find other S's around them. A B will find they are now with B's. Your frequencies will draw you to a system more like you than your previous system. You'll now get to hang out with folks more like yourself. Even when the rest of the system crashes, you can transform. And when the rest of the system transforms, you can crash.

The bad news in chaos is that we can't control the whole, the Event. The good news is that we can control ourselves, our Response. We do that by choosing how we react to situations. The simple equation is E + R = O.

Event + Response = Outcome

A simple memory tool for this is to remember that you are the (h)ERO of your own life's journey, because for every Event, it is your Response that decides the Outcome for you.

And there is always choice. You always have the free will to decide how you will react to what happens to you. Always.

For those who disagree, read <u>Man's Search for Meaning</u> by Victor Frankl. In the hell of a Nazi concentration camp, Frankl maintained his heart, his humanity and his life. Even surrounded by death and dehumization, we can choose how we meet it.

Choice

One of my first life teachers was Rev. Evan Hodkins. He talked about fate and free will in a metaphor that I now call the Loom of Life. Life is like a weaver's loom. The vertical, fixed strands of the warp are Fate. They are set in place in our lives and we cannot change them: taxes, death, earthquakes, wars and Acts of God. But life also gives us Free Will. We can choose the color, size, and texture of the yarn that we put on the shuttle to weave through the warp strands. Do we choose natural fiber or synthetic? Ribbons or plastic? How often do we go into the vertical 'givens', and how many do we glide over? The colors, patterns and quality of the final tapestry are the result of both destiny and our choices.

Figure 7

Loom of Life

Choice is the key. Over the years, I've become pretty good at manifesting. I know that my life depends on my choices, and on how clear, vivid and committed I am about those choices. My tutor in Manifestation 101 was a close friend, Norma Johnson (AllinSpirit.com). When I'd find myself in pain, I'd call Norma to help me design my way to something better in my life. I call her my Interior Designer. I always knew what I didn't want. "I don't want a man who: (fill in the blank) is sexist; is bigoted; is insecure; is needy; is overweight, lives in front of the TV, etc., etc., etc."

Norma would smile after I listed each complaint. She'd quietly say, "So, what do you want?" And she'd stick with me until I could say in positive words what I did want: "I want a man who loves my emotions, brain, body and spirit. I want a man who responds to people based on who they are inside. I want a man who knows that what he puts in his mouth determines what his body looks like. I want a man who is open-minded, playful, exploring, creative . . . who likes cats."

Now, my Norma-mantra back to myself every time I'm dissatisfied, is, quietly, "What do I want?"

The home I had in Puerto Rico was a direct result of choosing what I wanted long before the explosion point, and staying focused intently on exactly what I wanted in my next home which I knew I wanted to be in the Caribbean.

The Australian Aborigines use a similar approach to life. What I know of their way of life comes from the experience of Marlo Morgan, a sister Kansan who I've had the pleasure of meeting. (I highly recommend her books Mutant Message and Message from Forever.) I doubt that the Aborigines call it manifestation. They might call it positive focus. The Aborigines don't waste their time or precious energy being against something. They know that you give power to what you focus on, negatively or positively. They chose what they do want to have happen and then work for that. I love a quote from the Dalai Lama. He says, "I do not know whether our work (to free Tibet from the Communist Chinese) will prevail. I do not do it because I know we will succeed. I do it because it makes me feel good. It is the right thing for me to do."

One more word on the KMC. Stability is not 'bad'. It comes off in the model as the contributor to breakdown, but breakdown isn't 'bad' either. Ann Jaramillo, a Denver consultant and colleague, pointed out, "The parts in the breakdown pile recycle around and become ERI for another system somewhere else." And breakdown is a time that can be tremendously rich in learning. It is the quiet time, the retreat into the cave, the mountaintop, the lake. After we lick our wounds, we ask ourselves, "Where did I go wrong?" Better said, "What can I learn from this?" Because nature doesn't have Right/Wrong, Good/Bad, Should have/ Shouldn't have. Nature only has "What works?" And, as Meg Wheatley points out, it isn't even "What works best?" Nature doesn't care if it's the best solution. If it's a solution that works, nature uses it.

Quantum Life

I affect my reality. You affect your reality. Our world responds to us by giving to us what we expect to see. The observer is the observed.

A speck of light energy known as a photon will show up as either matter (particle) or energy (wave) depending on what the observer expects it to be. This speck of energy knows what it is expected to be and it becomes that. That means a photon is conscious. It's at this point that Niels Bohr's insight helps: "Those who are not amazed by quantum don't understand it." Susan Cravey, a friend of mine in Puerto Rico says, "Once you understand quantum, you realize that it's all possible. Anything is possible. Anything. And it's not pop psychology. It's Science telling us this."

The bottom line of quantum puts the responsibility for your life squarely on your shoulders. It is the end of the age of victimhood. What you have in your life is what you have created in your life. You have called it into your life, consciously or unconsciously, by your expectations, your desires, what you focus on. Your life is your making.

Be careful to avoid beating up on yourself when

sh---y things happen. When my personal journey with cancer showed up, I went into rage, denial, avoidance, terror, and yes, self-blame. Blame and shame are lousy motivators. My guiding question at times like this is from Oprah Winfrey. "What can I learn from this that I wouldn't have learned any other way?"

So guiding principles in the quantum world are

~ I am responsible for what I draw into my life;

and

~ What can I learn from this?

What Chaos Doesn't Do

Chaos provides us with the raw materials. Every piece of ERI that comes into our system gives us the opportunity to decide how to react. *There is no such thing as negative information in a system dedicated to learning and growing.* It gives us the chance to set in motion a pattern of behavior that will serve us or harm us. Every explosion is rich with new beginnings. Chaos stirs the pot, brings all the options to us and swirls them around us.

But chaos does not choose for us. We choose. The power of choice is our divine human birthright. We do have free will, and it does create our reality. In the midst of terror and panic, we can be tranquil. In the middle of hatred and violence, we can be calm and use our hearts. In ugliness, we can find beauty. In despair, we can trust.

The message of quantum is freeing and magnificent:

There is always choice. Always.

And it always counts. Always.

Summary - Chapter 3
Chaos

I. Chaos in Nature

A. Hurricane Lenny first hurricane from the east moving west

B. These are unprecedented times - we haven't seen anything like it before.

C. Quantum says that the unpredictable is rich with potential.

II. Dr. Ilya Prigogine's Theory of Dissipative Structures

A. Nobel Prize for Chemistry in 1977

B. Showed that systems can develop in an upward spiral of increased complexity, contrary to the Second Law of Thermodynamics (heat, on its own, only goes down the energy ladder).

C. Showed that chaos is a catalyst that allows systems to fall apart in order to come back together at a higher, more complex level.

III. Kirk Model of Chaos

A. Based on Dr. Prigogine's Theory of Dissipative Structures

B. KMC Part 1

1. Beginning of chaos cycle

2. ERI (Energy Rich Input) comes into the system and has nowhere to go

3. The loose ERI runs around and creates waves of agitation in the system

4. The waves bump into themselves (feedback) creating increased agitation.

C. KMC Part 2

1. Middle of cycle - tension's building

2. There is a range of reactions to the agitation (Equilibrium Scale)

a. Stability-seeking "S" reactions: minimum movement, maximum stagnation/entropy

b. Balance-seeking "B" reactions. maximum movement, minimum entropy

D. KMC Part 3

1. Explosion Point - Kablooie!

2. Agitation finally breaks the Tolerance Boundary and the system explodes.

3. Bifurcation point means the exploded system has 2 (bi) ways to go

a. Breakdown where the energy is released and scattered = wasted energy

b. Transformation where the energy reforms, attracts back to itself those elements vibrating at the higher, more complex level - new form is

*able to handle more ERI than
previous system.*

4. Classic example of those in the
railroad business (S folks) and
those in the transportation
business (B folks)

IV. The History of the Organism

A. "The history of the organism (system)
tends to be determinative at the
bifurcation point", according to Fritjof
Capra.

B. The system's history is the
actions/reactions that happen during
the Agitation (after ERI comes in and
before Explosion Point) . . . the space
between the goalposts - the vertical
bars in the KMC, the 'cooking time'.

C. Author as guinea pig: What emotional
patterns motivated the decisions that
resulted in breakdown?

D. The emotional patterns/ patterns of action
during the cooking time are the
system's history that can determine
whether it breaks down or transforms.

E. The system (personal or organizational)
can transform if the patterns are strong
enough to draw elements together
again after the explosion point.

F. Your own personal Chaos Model

V. Misfits in the System

A. Balance-seeking person in a Stability-seeking system

B. Stability-seeking person in a Balance-seeking system

C. At explosion, you get to join a group of people like yourself.

> 1. When an S system crashes, a B can transform.

> 2. When a B system transforms, an S person can crash.

VI. Choice

A. Event + Response = Outcome (You are the (h)ERO of your own life journey.)

B. Loom of Life

> 1. Free Will - the Choices of our divine birthright

> 2. Fate - the Givens

> 3. The final tapestry of our life is the weaving together of what fate gives us and what we choose to make of it.

C. Manifestation 101

> 1. What *do* I want?

> 2. What do *I* want?

> 3. What do I *want*?

VII. The Magic of Quantum

A. I affect my reality: the observer is the observed

B. Photons, basic elements of ELM energy, are conscious. They know what we are expecting or choosing and they become that.

C. End of the age of victimhood

D. Your life is your making

    1. Avoid self-blame

    2. What can I learn from this?

VII. It's All Choice

A. Chaos presents the options but doesn't choose

B. We choose, consciously or unconsciously, by our free will actions.

C. The message of <u>Quantum Lite</u>

    1. There is always choice. Always.

    2. Choice always counts. Always.

Chapter 4

Uniqueness

Amazing Grace

It is New Year's Day morning, year 2000. I've been on my writing sabbatical in St. Vincent for two months – have lived through Lenny and am waiting now to see if the electronic world has collapsed as predicted. In the predawn world I discover that my computer still runs, and my cottage has electricity. I see by the lights sparkling outside that the island does, too.

The luscious yellow pineapple lies in juicy irregular hunks on my cutting board. My first food of the new millennium. I take a deep breath, close my eyes and indulge in my first taste of the year 2000 . . . and the first pineapple I've had in over a decade. For Christmas, I'd had fresh tomatoes, another delicacy of landmark proportions. For years my stress level had turned every bite of acidic food into painful mouth sores. I simply didn't eat citrus or tomatoes and had given up drinking OJ. But when the ripe red tomatoes were placed in front of me on Christmas Day, I know I could eat them. Something in my body had changed.

By the time I was ready to leave St. Vincent after only three months, my body was telling me that this lifestyle and this climate were very healthy for me. Several minor physical complaints had healed without my focusing on them. Was it 'simply' the clean air, fresh local food, the tranquil environment, and the opportunity to do my writing?

Nothing else had changed. I'd been able to be very productive, more than completing my writing goal. I'd fallen in love with the Caribbean and the 'Trades' that blew through my cottage day and night. But the joy of eating fresh tomatoes and pineapple was the piéce de résistance.

The message from my body to my brain was loud and clear: If all this is so good for you, why are you leaving it to go back to a lifestyle that isn't? Why just give this to yourself three months every decade, or maybe two weeks a year?

I did some out-of-the-box thinking, and realized I could run my company from the Caribbean as well as from Boulder. Thanks to the wonders of telecommuting, I could live and work in the Caribbean. And I began the chain of events that would result in just that after a very full year of planning, work and trust.

During that year of transition from Boulder to the Caribbean, I faced the reality that running my company was a major source of stress. Did I want to go through all the trouble of a move just to carry that stress to a prettier place? I felt like I'd been an overachiever since fourth grade. Did I have the courage to walk away from my CEO/lawyer identity to become a writer? Did I have enough faith in myself to face the financial risk of no income for an unknown extended period of time? And, scariest of all, would anyone want to read my writing if I gave it all up and opted for the life of a writer?

I accepted the reality of what I knew in my heart: I was complete with my life in Boulder. My beautiful home on Ithaca Drive still echoed the absence of Frank. The company he founded which was a crowning glory in his life was not prospering under my leadership. My mother had died shortly after Frank. My daughter and Frank's children had long been adults and on their own. My ties to the US and my sisters could be nurtured from the Caribbean. There was nothing other than inertia holding me back . . . and of course, fear of the unknown.

So I set out to manifest my next home. I began my list of what I wanted (á la Norma).

What I Want in My Next Home

1. Constant Caribbean Trade Winds

2. On a small hill overlooking the water with views of green and trees

3. Small home (maximum of 1500 square feet) with 2 to 3 bedrooms

4. Open architecture with cathedral ceilings so breeze flows through the house; tile floors and tile roof (Spanish/Mediterranean style)

5. Yard with flowering bushes and fruit trees

6. Sense of peace and solitude. If I have neighbors, they're quiet and hidden from view

7. Within my price range

8. New construction (within 5 years)

9. Within ten minutes from grocery store, bank, gas station, etc.

10. Near, but not on, the water with a sandy swimming beach within 5-minute walk

11. Within 1 ½ hours of a major airport

I spent hours on the web researching Caribbean Islands and Central America's Caribbean coast. I found that many of the islands made land ownership for gringos difficult. It was either legally too complex, politically too risky or financially exorbitant -- inflated by cute little things like a 'mandatory new resident's license' of $50,000.

I added to my list:

12. Full legal ownership is easily available and guaranteed

For my taste, Belize's coastline was too flat. Costa Rica's Caribbean shoreline is all marshes and the trade winds don't blow on the Pacific side. Check off Belize and Costa Rica.

On the web I found a home for sale that seemed to fit all my criteria. It was in Dominica, a small mountainous island of rainforests in the central Caribbean. I flew to Dominica with a friend, and we explored the house and the island. I remember taking off from Dominica to return to Boulder. The noise of the propellers drowned out my sobs. I was terrified by the thought of moving to Dominica. Too many things didn't fit. But I was one month away from putting my home on the market and was already training the company's new leader. I felt hemmed in by my own momentum. When we landed in Martinique, my friend took me by the shoulders and said "Look, you don't have to move to Dominica. Give yourself permission to keep looking. You'll find what you want." By the time we got back to Boulder, my panic had subsided.

Dominica had clarified some basic requirements I'd left out. My self discoveries were an embarrassment. I considered myself to have a simple, non-materialistic lifestyle. Had this been true, Dominica would probably have appealed to me. But I had to swallow my pride and admit that I was indeed a jaded American. And my list grew longer.

13. At least 3 excellent restaurants (with fresh vegetables and dark green salads) within 20 minutes;

14. At least one Walmart / Target type store within 30 minutes (Ah, yes, Consumer's Anonymous!);

15. Marked highways with shoulders, free of potholes that I'll enjoy driving on;

16. Easily available technology and expertise to support my internet and computer systems;

17. A large island (over 70 miles long) with fields and meadows where I'll feel a sense of open space. (I had felt claustrophobic in Dominica's totally mountainous smallness.)

I had realized how critical it is to my happiness to have excellent restaurants, discount stores, good highways and quality technological support. And I'd discovered another basic need: friends of the heart. I have known that I am a person who is nurtured by a quiet life. But in Dominica's frontier-like geography, I realized that close friends would be 1 to 2 hours away over torturous mountain roads. So, the list grew:

18. Within 15 minutes, at least 3 good women friends and 2 good spiritual friends.

In several of the places I'd been in the Caribbean, I'd felt the friction of the cultural/racial/social class differences between the expats (Americans living abroad) and the locals. There were places where for very good reasons the locals felt bitter. Underneath a thin layer of politeness, they either barely concealed their resentment or were outright hostile. A lot of the expats lived with big dogs, behind walls, or in gated communities, sometimes with the wealthy locals.

I wanted a community where I could feel comfortable and enhanced with the cultural differences, not depressed or threatened by them. One crusty pioneer in a rural area of Dominica had told me, "Of course, you'll have to carry your cutlass (machete) and know how to use it. They have to know that you'll use it. I've bloodied more than one of them for coming at me." She offered to teach me the cutlass. Ah, yes. Another point of clarification:

19. I want a comfortable and cooperative spirit between myself and the local people -- a sense of mutual respect and gratitude for each other.

And finally, being a systems thinker, I asked myself, "What's the one description that encompasses it all?"

20. I want a home and environment that nurtures me, where I am productive, delighted, increasingly free of stress . . . healthy and excited about life.

Somewhere along the way, I'd made a sketch of my ideal home. I wanted every room to have a view of the ocean, so it ended up being a semi-circle.

List in hand, and with clarified intent, I went back to my drawing board, the Internet. I found the US Virgins, the BVI (British Virgins) and Puerto

Rico. The BVI and the USVI all looked pretty small, so I focused on Puerto Rico.

All I knew of Puerto Rico came from West Side Story. I set aside the prejudices that came to mind when I heard "Puerto Rican", and delved into a study of what was the front runner for my new home. I found that Puerto Rico has the highest per capita income of the Caribbean islands. This translated for me into a large middle and upper class of locals, less abject poverty and therefore less division between the Haves and Have-nots. Colonized by the Spanish over 500 years ago, their western civilization pre-dated that of the US. Now, as a US territory, they used the dollar, had the rights of US citizens, and land ownership was as straightforward as in the States. It was big enough (110 miles by 40 miles) and had gentle coastlines. Even a rainforest! And it had two central mountain ranges. (Well, they called them mountains. But at 1,000 meters or 3,000 feet, no self-respecting Coloradoan would call them anything other than big foothills.) English was taught in school, though Spanish was predominant. Lots of good beaches, a benign coast (no sharks, etc.), and a climate between 75 and 95 year-round. True, there was an occasional hurricane, but always with days of advance notice.

One of my wisdom teachers had warned me against looking for Paradise. "No place in the world is perfect. Every place has its blemishes. And wherever you go, you take yourself (and your issues) with you." So, it was a matter of deciding whether the blemishes of Puerto Rico were ones that I and my issues could live with.

Because the island was so big, I had to decide where to start looking for my home. By process of elimination, I decided on the northwest part of the island. I settled on the area between two towns with the exotic names of Arecibo and Mayagüez to begin my quest. I made reservations to spend two weeks in Puerto Rico to confirm that it would be my next home, and to find my house.

After landing in San Juan and driving all afternoon, I got to my guest house in the dark. I liked what I'd experienced on the way: friendly people, lush green mountains, spectacular ocean vistas.

The next morning at first light I ran out to the beach and into the water – briefly. I was immediately drug down by the 'undertoad' (as Frank called it.) Sputtering sand and amazement, I struggled to the shore and absorbed my first island girl lesson: a surfing beach doth not a swimming beach make!

Swimming out for the day, I set out to find the Puerto Rican realtor that my sister had connected me with. I was hopelessly lost for hours despite detailed maps and an advanced degree in map-reading. Puerto Rico had wasted no extra money on highway signs, and my very basic Spanish wasn't helping. The glow was beginning to wear off the island.

I found myself at a payphone outside a very seedy bar. Definitely one of the blemishes. The phone wouldn't accept my coins or my credit card, and the recorded messages were all in Spanish. Nothing was working for me. I was grimy and sweaty. The sun was glaring down on me; sand flies were feasting on my legs. The stench of urine in the phone booth was suffocating me. I was alone and lost. I didn't know a soul and didn't speak the language. I was exhausted, overwhelmed and depressed. All my demons surfaced and attacked. Was this just another wild dream taking me to the Moscow of the Caribbean? I felt like crying.

After what seemed like hours, I managed to get connected to my sister's office in Boulder. I prayed she'd be there. When I heard Jan's voice on the phone, I did cry. I felt like someone drowning whose hand has just been clasped with a firm grip from above.

With Jan's help, I did find my Puerto Rican realtor that day. But she left for her annual trip to France two days later, so I continued with another realtor, and on my own. I told everyone I met what kind of house I was looking for. Three people within two days told me, "You've got to go see Becky's house."

Indeed, Becky's house was the one. It was a wooden two-story dodecagon – a 12 sided 'round' house. The main living area was on the second floor. I walked up a set of wooden steps that curved around the outside of the house and stepped into a screened lanai with a breath-taking view of the Caribbean only 100 yards away. I stood in the treetops – looking out through a canopy of leaves. Two huge guardian trees stood, one on each side of the house. A Mahogany tree on the right and a Mango on the left. I could see only trees and ocean. No houses. There was a peace and tranquility about the house that belied its closeness to the road.

The house had been built by Becky and Bill with love, master craftsmanship and ecological care. It had gone through the direct hit of Hurricane

George with only a scratch. It fit everything on the list except there was no red tile roof, and it was 8 years old instead of 5.

I immediately liked Becky. She felt like kin. She was a writer and an environmental advocate. She moved slowly and rhythmically and spoke thoughtfully. She was quiet, humorous and intuitive.

It took Becky and me a week to negotiate our agreement on the house. I well remember the night before I was to hand Becky the earnest money. I was staying at the Lazy Parrot and was awake most of the night: reviewing lists, endlessly refiguring finances. I was excited, but mostly I was scared. Was I making a mistake? What had I not thought of? If only I had a partner, someone to share the weight of the decision. I'd never bought a house on my own before.

The chasm between my comfort zone and what I was about to do was a big one. I had used all my considerable mental abilities trying to construct a 100% safe scenario. But to no avail. I was still plagued with dozens of "What if's?" A list, even a long one, of factual realities does not bridge over the river of fears to the other side. In my heart I knew that the leap across the chasm can't be made in the mind. Getting to a place of trust is not a mental journey. Faith is not created by logic. There is a point beyond which the power of the mind cannot take us. I was at that point. And at that point, one either clings to the safety of the known, or steps out into the unknown. I remembered a poem given to me by a friend years before when I was leaving to live in Moscow.

Faith

When you have come to the edge

of all the light you know,

and are ready to step into the darkness,

one of two things will happen.

You will find solid ground

under your feet,

or

you will be taught

how to fly.

The next morning I handed the check to Becky. It was the first irreversible step I had taken toward my new life. I flew back to Boulder, sold and packed my home, transferred ownership of my company and brought closure to all the other aspects of my life in Colorado – all in 5 weeks. The timing was tight. Definite breakdown at one point: I was in tearful hyper-stress by the moving van's last minute notice that their payment (several thousand dollars) needed to be in cash the next morning or they wouldn't come pack me out of my house. I had new owners moving in the following day. But there was a flow to most of it that felt like a continuing affirmation.

In the pre-dawn darkness of a snowy Christmas morning, December 25, 2000, carrying Maya in her cat box, I left Boulder. I touched down in San Juan near midnight. I was tired but excited about beginning this new phase in my life.

In Becky's last conversation with me, she had said, "You're living in grace, Phyllis." I asked her what she meant. She went on to tell me, "The morning we signed the agreement and you gave me the check, about an hour later, I got a phone call from a man in San Juan. He'd been interested in the house. He asked me what had been wrong with our phones. I said, 'Nothing. We've been getting calls just fine.' He said he'd been trying to call for three days and got recordings saying our line was out of service. He was ready to buy the house and was calling with an offer. I told him the house was sold."

"You were supposed to have this house, Phyllis. When I first met you in the driveway, a voice in my head said, 'She's the one.' Living in grace means that when you are doing the work you came to do, you can do no wrong. It's what the Buddhists call living your Dharma. When you are on your path, whatever happens to you resolves itself for your benefit. You are on your path."

Quantum Grace

Living your uniqueness is living in grace. Grace is the way the quantum Universe honors those who are contributing their uniqueness to the Whole. We can't make grace happen. It's an indirect outcome of the way we chose to live our life. The opposite of grace is force. Force has been the main verb in my vocabulary most of my life.

The first half of my life had been about constructing my world to give me security and status. At the height of my career as a rising star with the Solicitor's Office I was seeing a therapist twice a week. I have Dr. Jeff Raff, a Jungian counselor in Denver, to thank for setting me on my path to uniqueness . . . and preserving my sanity. I remember Jeff telling me that Carl Jung said that a person doesn't really become an individual (individuate) until age thirty-five or forty. Until that time, we pattern ourselves after what our parents want or what society sells us under the Success brand.

It wasn't until after (or because of?) my first huge failure as a trial lawyer at age 35 that I even began to ask myself "How can I be happy?" instead of "How can I be successful?"

I spent my whole life making things happen that I wanted to have happen. And I was proud of my batting average. Not happy. Just proud of my résumé.

One day when my mother was visiting me in Moscow, she quietly said to me, "I've never understood why you struggle so." It was a shock to me that mother thought I struggled a lot. I thought I lived a very normal life. Don't you have to push to get things done? How am I going to get what I want unless I make it happen? Of course, all my efforts to 'make it happen' weren't deeply satisfying, even when 'it' did happen. And then some catastrophe (better known as chaos) would come along. I'd realize that my success neither kept my world stable nor made me happy.

But it wasn't until chaos theory and quantum that I began to understand why.

The joke is, the way you really *do* in the quantum world, is *not to do*. It is to *be*. And the better you *be,* the more you allow the world to *do for you.* Quantum is a set-up. The quantum life is one of co-creation. It's a partnership between you and "whatever it is that's out there" to quote Einstein. Like any relationship, one partner can't do it all. Or if they do, the result is less than satisfactory for both parties.

Think about it. You can't possibly do the exact action that will result in getting you what you want. You simply have no way of knowing all the twists and turns, the chain reactions that chaos will throw in your path between your starting point A and your desired outcome point Z.

What you *can* do is *be the vibration* that will attract to you what you want. The object is to feel the experience of what you want to create. That feeling literally becomes a vibrational flag. You are planting the energetic flag. And that flag broadcasts. The clearer you feel/see/hear/think/taste what it is that you want, the stronger the flag broadcasts what it is that you want. That's why guided imagery, affirmations, and clear intention all work. Current research seems to indicate that this is how prayer, or prayer intention works. (Read The Isaiah Effect by Greg Braden.) Planting the flag is like striking middle C on the piano. It puts other similar tones in motion. The flag sends out the energetic message of what you want. Then, through the swirling energies around you, that energetic broadcast attracts other similar energies to you. Remember how entrainment and magnetic attraction work?

Figure 1:
You in the Quantum Soup

And below is You Planting the Flag of your Focus

The Quantum Soup mix is present in the
background, but the focused

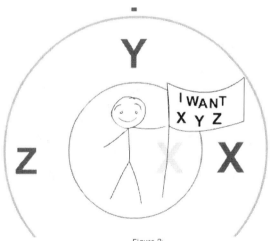

Figure 2:
You Planting the Flag

clarity of You Planting the Flag dominates the
vibrations

Understand that if you want to live your quantum uniqueness, then 'You' is a verb. As my wise friend Norma said to me recently, "Our 'things', our projects, our professions in life are just where we focus our actions. They're not really what we're about. What we're really about is discovering the bigger realm of who we are."

Your unique contribution strengthens the system. In return the system supports you. The world responds when you announce to it what is special about you, what you want, what you are committed to. This is exactly what Sir William Murray discovered when he made up his mind to form a Himalayan Expedition in the late 1800's. It has become known as the Commitment quote.

Until one is committed

there is hesitancy, the chance to draw back, always ineffectiveness.

Concerning all acts of initiative and creation

there is one elementary truth,

the ignorance of which kills countless ideas and splendid plans:

that the moment one definitely commits oneself,

then Providence moves, too.

All sorts of things occur to help one

that would otherwise never have occurred.

A whole stream of events issues from the decision,

raising in one's favor

all manner of unforeseen incidents and meetings and material assistance, which no one could have dreamt would have come their way.

I think of commitment as planting the flag. I see Joan of Arc standing on the hilltop with the French Fleur de Lis whipping in the wind. She stood there alone, planted her flag in the ground and declared to the world what she stood for. And by golly, people who believed in the same thing rallied around her. Stating your unique commitment is planting the energetic flag.

A good marketer knows that when you want to sell something, it isn't just about finding the *largest* audience. It's about finding the *best* audience – those who are most likely to want your product. In the past, we've spent lots of time and money supporting Madison Avenue to do polls. We strategize based on market analyses. What if there was a way to use the 'magic' of the energetic network? One of the best energetic networks we now have is the Internet. An energetic network automatically selects your market; based on the unique vibration you've put out there—your USP, or Unique Selling Proposition.

Your USP is the one thing that people can remember about the product or experience a year later. In more personal terms, what one thing makes you unique as a person? What will someone remember about you a year after meeting you? In marketing, it's more popularly known as your niche. When the energetic network is vibrating with your USP, it's doing the work of Madison Avenue with less time and more efficiently. It culls out the deadbeats and clowns, and delivers to you the gems you want. The people who want you will find you based on their attraction to your uniqueness. They show up at your flag. It pulls into your path those 'unforeseen incidents and meetings and material assistance' that will support you. It isn't really magic. It's science. It's how energy works.

Besides, it's more fun and a lot easier to use energy to help you. Have you ever been at a critical point in a project where you know if you just push a little harder, it'll happen? For example, you're a realtor and the 'right' buyer has just called to say they'll be back into town to buy that ranch. The trouble is, you have non-refundable tickets for a trip you've promised yourself and your family that you *will* take. The prospective buyer will be in town while you're gone, of course. You're a single mom, and your commission would get your son through his first year in college. What do you do?

I have a close realtor friend who experiences this kind of conflict occasionally. It's familiar to most of us who are dedicated to our careers. When my friend faces these obvious conflicts between work and personal goals, she usually follows her commitment to herself to take the vacation. And, upon her return, the ranch sale takes place anyway – without her hands-on orchestration in the meantime. Why? How does it work?

Is it possible that the energetic flags that we plant continue to broadcast in our absence, lining up events that give us the results we want? Is it possible that if it's divine appointment for 'right' family to buy 'right' ranch, it will happen, with or without our continued presence? The realtor has done her part in skillfully matching prospective buyer and sale property. She has long ago 'done her work' in developing her intuition about what a buyer family really needs even when they don't know what they want. She senses when a buyer and a home are made for each other. Her real work is done in making the match, and then, sometimes, getting out of the way. In addition to allowing the buyer-energy and property-energy to do their own dance, going on vacation is a perfect way to strengthen yourself. Leave the doing behind and be in the being for awhile.

Often the harder we push, the more elusive the goal becomes. Did you ever experience the Magic Eye phenomenon that was big in the US in the mid-1990's? It is the computer-generated, random-dot stereogram that 'magically' becomes 3-dimensional IF you allow your eyes to perform certain feats. To get this unaided (no 3-D glasses) stereovision to work, you must be able to see without looking. It's definitely Zen. You have to let your eyes unfocus and get blurry and stare blankly at an object without looking at it. When your eyes arrive at the magic point, the object rises out of the flat 2 dimensional page into 3 dimensional life. It's an incredibly cool experience. And, it is hugely frustrating to Type A personalities who get to their goals by hard work and pushing.

Frank became enamored with Magic Eye books. We had them on our Executive Toys table in the workshops. He was delighted that they were the original work of Dr. Bela Julesz (You-lish), a fellow Bell Labs scientist. They had taken the world by storm. I loved watching the Type A's try to conquer the Magic Eye, doing exactly what I'd done when I first encountered it — trying to force it or solve it intellectually.

Magic Eye was introduced to Frank and me after a workshop in Nebraska by Jim Dutton. He was the training director at Nebraska Public Power District. Jim and Frank, having discovered that they had similar intelligence profiles, had become good buddies.

Jim couldn't wait to show Frank the latest toy he'd discovered in a mall shop. Jim said it had taken him days to 'see 3-D'. Therefore, I was going to see it within minutes, I told myself. An hour later, Jim and Frank drug me out of the store in a serious state of disbelief and anger. I couldn't 'make' the *%^!_)@+)$*$&*#!!!!* thing work. We left the shop with a huge framed picture of dots that was supposed to be a dinosaur. That dinosaur didn't rise up out of the swamp for me for weeks. But it was a wild experience when it did! I still love doing the Magic Eye things. (For those of you who missed the Magic Eye and are up for a quantum exercise, order the book *SuperStereogram* by David Burder.)

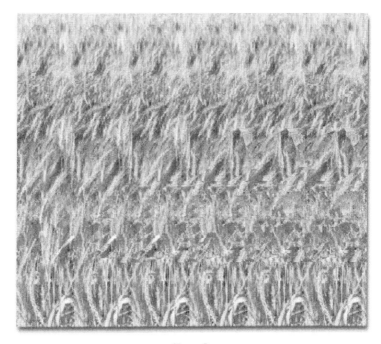

Figure 3:
"Eagle in Flight" stereograph
© 1993-1995 Timothy Ecket.

My point here is that it is our way of *being* in the world, not our *doing*, that matters (no pun intended), quantumly speaking. And the Magic Eye was a test that most of us doers failed until we could simply relax, allow our eyes to make their own adjustment, and let another reality come to us. It is a reality that happens only by letting go. It happens by moving into a Theta type of state where we allow the brain to self-organize into a new pattern that can accommodate the new energy-rich input. For the achievers of the industrialized left-brained world, that type of release as a way of doing/being is very foreign to us. And, after all, it is the left brain and the doers that have gotten us to where we are: the most powerful and richest nation in perhaps all of history. Pretty good success story. So what's wrong with being a left-brained doer? Nothing. Unless it doesn't work anymore. Remember that nature is only concerned with what works and what doesn't, not with 'right' and 'wrong'.

Professor Peter Senge is the Director of the Organizational Learning Center at the Sloan School of Management at MIT and author of The Fifth Discipline. He has been named a 'Strategist of the Century' by the *Journal of Business Strategy*, and is one of 24 men and women who have 'had the greatest impact on the way we conduct business today'. He has studied how firms and organizations develop adaptive capabilities. He might be someone pretty good at spotting a big system trend. Peter Senge says,

> "It is the characteristics
> that have gotten us to where we are
> that now threaten to kill us."

So if left-brained-making-it-happen is what got us to the top and is now threatening to kill us, what might be the adaptive capability we need to develop now? If chaos can always mess up our best-laid plans, what do we do? How do we *be* in the chaos so our being ends up productive? What might be a Quantum response for the Newtonian fix we find ourselves in?

Honey-Money

Bucky Fuller has the best answer to this that I've found. He pondered the question of how to *be* productively in the world, and came up with the scientific explanation of the way reality worked for him. He called it 'Honey-Money'. More scientifically, it's called orthogonality or the precessional effect. Orthogonal means something that happens at right angles to something else. Precession is when the *direction of movement* ends up being at a right angle from the *direction that the force was applied*.

In very simple terms and loosely translated, Bucky said that *Universe supports you, indirectly,* based on you doing your unique work in the world. He observed this in nature and found it to be a generalized principle. Secondly, he found that Universe supports you IF you are doing what needs to be done. So the issue becomes determining what needs to be done as well as what you want to do and have the unique talent to do.

Bucky described precession as the effect of bodies in motion on other bodies in motion. It's like a spinning top where the force put on it to make it spin makes it move in a direction different from the original force. Bucky called this principle Honey-Money. He used the metaphor of bees and flowers to explain how Honey-Money works for humans.

In the picture below, Mr. Bee wants nectar to make honey. He finds a flower crawls inside, does his nectar collecting dance. He 'accidentally' gets dusted with pollen. He goes on to the next flower where he does the same dance. This time he shakes off some of the pollen. In the process of dancing around through the flowers sucking nectar, he 'accidentally' cross-pollinates the field of flowers. This results in the continued growth of flowers. This 'accident' in turn, gives him a secure long term future source of honey, and also gives a valuable service to nature.

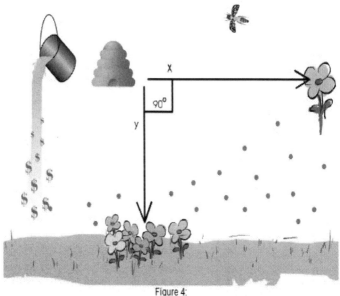

Figure 4:
Bucky Fuller's Honey-Money

Bucky says, "Humans as Honey-Money seeking bees, do many of nature's required tasks, only inadvertently. *Our individually programmed survival instincts result in that which supports us, but indirectly and from a different direction than the one we put our energy toward.*" (italics added)

You can read Bucky's own words for a fuller explanation -- no pun intended -- of the precessional effect in the appendix following this chapter's Summary. Bucky isn't easy to read. He said he'd rather be not understood than misunderstood. He goes to great and wordy lengths to get his idea across – often creating new words in the process. Despite that, reading Bucky's own words is a good way to get to know this amazing man. (Critical Path) If reading Bucky's own words is as hard for you as it is for me, go to the very readable Cliff Notes on Bucky: Buy Lloyd Sieden's book Buckminster Fuller's Universe: His Life and Work, with a great forward by Norman Cousins.

Bucky experimented with and came to rely on these 'side effects' of an action rather than on direct actions. As a true humanist, Bucky's goal was not wealth, awards or fame, though he ended up with all of them. His goal was to create 'artifacts for humanity'. Those are inventions to raise the standard of living for all people. Bucky would find something that he felt needed to be done which no one else was doing that he had the ability to do. He would then do that job with the faith that he, his project and his family would be supported if his venture was in fact needed. Fuller seldom concerned himself with direct support, such as payment for inventing a particular artifact. Instead, he put his focus on the project, knowing that "seemingly indirect support would come from a regenerative Universe which always supports required actions." He found that support generally appeared only at the last instant and from unexpected sources. In my life, I have seen the same thing. I call it gifts from the J.I.T. (just in time) Universe. Nerve-racking for we humans who are engrained with long-term planning.

As we contribute our unique gifts to the world at large (the big system), it is strengthened. Remember? Diversity enhances systems. You get to follow your bliss, be your special self, and get support doing it. This is what Marsha Sinetar says in her book Do What You Love, the Money Will

<u>Follow: Discovering Your Right Livelihood</u>. My favorite chapter in this practical and inspirational book is "Work as Love, Work as Devotion." The more naturally passionate you are about your work, the stronger are the energetic vibrations you put into the world. The stronger those vibrations, the more nature will respond with support. It can't help it. It's a law of energy.

Bucky was a master at being his unique self, contributing his unique gifts and allowing Universe to support him. From this perspective, it is not just your joy, it is your job in the world to be your unique self.

One of my favorite Star Trek scenes is from the movie *The First Contact*. It's where Jean Luc Picard gives us a glimpse of one of our possible futures. In the movie, Jean Luc of the 24th Century is having a conversation with Lillie from Earth's year 2063. Thanks to a timewarp. Lillie is on board the star ship Enterprise and being given a tour by Jean Luc. She is in awe of the amount of Titanium in the ship.

Figure 5: Jean Luc Picard and Lily
© 1998 Paramount Pictures.

Lily: How big is this ship?

Picard: There are 24 decks. Almost 700 meters long.

Lily: It took me six months to scrounge up enough Titanium just to build a four-meter cockpit! How much did this thing cost?!

Picard: The economics of the future are somewhat different. You see, money doesn't exist in the 24th Century.

Lily: No money? You mean you don't get paid!

Picard: The acquisition of wealth is no longer the driving force in our lives. We work to better ourselves and the rest of humanity.

If indeed quantum is inviting us to a future where our societies flourish based on our

contributions of our best selves, what are the baby
steps we begin to take now? How can we learn to be
the bee in the Honey-Money scenario? How can we
learn to co-create with quantum grace in our lives
instead of forcing our way in the world? Do we
hang out like hippies; go 'back to the land' and raise
organic fruits and nuts; dance around to Bobbi
McFerrin's *Don't Worry! Be Happy*??? How do we
find that Balance far from equilibrium where
quantum grace kicks in to support us and our work?

7 Steps to Beeing

Being yourself is the force that makes things
happen. The stronger you are about you, the more
Universe shows up with support.

Getting support in the Honey-Money game
comes from being the bee. And if you're conscious
about the process like Bucky was, it's more fun.
The following baby steps are what my experiments
have taught me. They are offered to you as my
experience. The quantum dance is a Balance of the
quiet-receptive-intentional-internal and the
attentive-responsive-active-external. You can do
them and see if they work for you. See if you feel
"Providence move, too."

Step # 1

1. Know your uniqueness.
Socrates said, "Know Thyself." Figure
out what is special about you. There's
only one of you, and you're here to be
that one. The big system, Divine
Oneness nurtures you as you nurture it
by contributing the special stuff you are

*made of. Knowing your purpose(s) here
is critical to your happiness.*

When I came home after three years in
Russia, I was a basket case. I was depressed and
exhausted in every way: physically, mentally,
emotionally, and spiritually. The excitement and
challenge of treading water 36 hours a day for 3
years had taken its toll. Back home in Boulder in
the shelter of my sister's home, I went into an
emotional cave for almost a year. I didn't want to
see or talk to anyone other than my sister and
nephew. My bedroom window looked out over a
meadow and lake to the foothills. I would lie there
for hours just looking out the window. I was dead
inside. I remember feeling like I would never feel
joy again in my life. I could breathe, eat and sleep
and walk – and that was about it.

I was also quietly terrified about my future. I
knew I could never again be a lawyer. The thought
of dressing in a suit and walking into corporate
mentality literally nauseated me. I would get a
sinking feeling in the pit of my stomach every time
I even drove past a law office. I also knew I could
never return to being a classroom teacher again.
Both of my previous careers were out of the
question. What kind of job could I possibly do? I
only sunk further into despair when I thought about
any job that might be available nearby. I remember
swearing to myself that I would never again
prostitute myself to a paycheck. I would find work I
honestly loved, or . . . or what? I didn't know. I
wasn't ready to die, but there absolutely was no
alternative to doing work that my heart would
treasure. And in the back of my mind there was

always the soft ticking of my diminishing savings account, fueling the quiet panic.

Then, one day I had a conversation with someone where I felt alive. It was a small spark, but in my darkness it felt big. What had we been talking about that made me feel alive? Then another conversation. Then an article in the paper caught my interest. I decided to start a list. I began writing down everything that made a blip on the screen for me. As I began to come back to life, I wrote down every positive, life-giving event:

- What subjects interested me?
- Who did I like to talk to?
- What did I enjoy reading about?
- What places did I like to go to?
- When I felt myself being animated, what was I talking about?
- What lit my fire?

Every time there was a flicker, I put it on my list. I remember looking at my list one day and thinking to myself, "This doesn't look like a job description to me." But I remember that I felt humor about that, not despair.

Shortly after that, one morning in September, I awoke and looked out over the lake. I knew that I was ready to come out of the cave. It was that simple. After breakfast, I sat on my bed and had a long meditation. I had my list in front of me. I said to Divine Oneness, "I'm ready to be in the world again. I don't know what I'm going to do. I don't know what I'm able to do. But here on this list is what I want to do. I need help. Please help me find work that will make my heart sing."

Two hours later the phone rang. It was Gail Hoag, a casual acquaintance through mutual friends who had worked with me in Moscow. She said, "I've gotten excited about an idea that's just come to me. I want to know if you'd be interested in working on it with me?" Gail and I ended up forming Changing Pathways, Inc. to do training on organizational change. During that time, we exchanged workshops with BCAL, the Boulder Center of Accelerative Learning. My BCAL workshop changed my life. I remember being in the workshop and being so charged with excitement that I couldn't stay in my seat. It was like every cell in my body was yelling "Yes!" My swinging compass needle had locked on true north. I had found the material that I wanted to work with for life. I did not know that I had also found the man who would be my life partner. A few months later, Frank invited me to join BCAL as his co-facilitator. The rest, so to speak, is history. I had set foot on the path. I knew I was home.

"You were born unique.

Don't die a copy."

-- Anonymous

Here are some exercises to help you begin defining your uniqueness. Get your journal, find a quiet corner and explore the bigger picture of who you are.

- What have you always wanted to do?
- If you won the lottery, what would you do with your days?

- What can you get so involved in that you lose track of time?
- What have you always wanted to study?
- If you could spend a year as an apprentice with someone living, dead or fictional, who would that be?
- What are your all-time favorite movies? What characters did you feel most like? Why?
- What five books have had the strongest impact on you? What were they about?
- Spend some time online and browse career choice sites. Take some of the free online assessment tests.
- Ask your friends and family to give you 5 to 10 descriptive words for you. Then ask them, "If you could see me starring in another career role, what would it be?"
- Read Do What You Love, the Money Will Follow.

Step # 2

2. *Be you. Ask yourself, "Am I really doing my thing? Am I contributing my uniqueness to the Whole? Am I engaged with life in a way that adds the specialness of who I am? Or am I busy 'earning a living' doing something to merely survive? Am I afraid to change? Am I afraid to leave what I think gives me security?"*

This is a story of Al Lemieux. I first met Al when he did our workshop. He was an Assistant Principal in an excellent school system. He had a respectable track record with some fairly prestigious schools. He brought teachers from his system to the workshops, and I could tell he was loved and respected. Al is one of the most widely read and experienced educators I know. Whenever a new philosophy, program, or educator arrives on the scene, Al goes into absorption mode. He researches and does his best to actually experience the new concept. He then makes his own objective analysis about its effectiveness and validity. He is free and diverse about what he synthesizes into his own practice. He is virtually a walking encyclopedia of education for others.

Al came to Frank's 65th birthday party. He made a toast to Frank that went something like this. "I've wanted to change what I'm doing for some time now. I've wanted to step out of traditional education and begin pursuing some independent paths. I've made the decision to do that, and I want you to know that it's your fault!"

Al was taking a courageous move to follow his bliss. He was in a system at a time when many would have 'just hung on until retirement.' He was married and raising his second family. Al is a man who takes his obligations seriously, and he had financial responsibilities to two families. He and DeAnna had taken time to plan how the transition would happen, but there was no immediate replacement for the security of his regular paycheck from the school district. Why did he do it?

Al said, "You just have to get out of the box, or you continue to do the same thing over and over.

We just weren't getting anywhere under the existing way of doing things. When I got it about whole brain learning, that you can get three times the amount of learning, I knew I had to be somewhere that I could teach that way. If a place didn't exist, then I'd have to create one. I knew I had to go out there and find and be with people who were doing it a different way."

"If you never do it, take that step out of the box, then you face the pain of not being true to yourself. I've taken those kinds of risks before. I know that one of the things I love and do well is bringing people into a place of positive consensus. I've stepped out in my life and done that, gotten people's trust in the process and achieved some victories. Yes, being out there like that involves a risk – going against the grain, speaking out when you see injustice, taking the long view instead of going for immediate gratification. It can be hard. But the really dangerous risk is the one of not doing it – of not staying true to who you are."

Being true to who you are may mean choosing a new reality for yourself: a new employer, yourself as your employer, new friends, new surroundings. You can choose a new reality from all the possibilities that exist right now for you in the quantum soup. It's important to be compassionate with yourself at the same time you are courageous about the change you are calling in to your life. Realize that you have had the job, or whatever it is you're changing, because it has served you. Until now. Avoid judgment and avoid going into victim mentality. Simply accept that it has worked for you in the past, and now you are ready to move on to something more fulfilling. Start making your choices about now.

Step # 3

3. *Be clear about what you want. Remember the most basic of energy photons are conscious: If you ask for a wave, you get a wave. If you ask for a particle you get a particle. Conscious energy responds to what you ask for, so be clear.*

When I was in kindergarten in Manifestation School, one of the first things I learned was: You get what you ask for so be clear about what you want. Remember that the clerk at Universal Fulfillment Center who's filling your order follows directions and doesn't make assumptions. If the clerk gets an order for candles, you'll get candles. So when 12 bright red thin tapers arrive, you can't wail, "But I wanted 12 yellow short column candles!!" If color and shape are important, ya gotta be specific. On the other hand, if color and shape aren't important, and you like to be surprised, then leave those categories open. I find that the less you load your requests with trivial details, the faster your request will produce results.

Use both your right and left brain for this. Your left brain will give you the words and concepts. It will help you put together all the information you got in Step #1. It will help you form ideas about possible directions you might go, places you might search.

Then bring in your right brain. Make your ideas multi-sensory. Remember, the strength of the response you get out of the quantum soup depends on the vividness of the message you send out. Clear and intense thoughts broadcast highly magnetic messages. Put your order out to Universe detailed with sights, sounds, smells, tastes, feelings. For refreshers, go back to where I talk about Norma as my interior designer (near the Loom of Life).

Then your whole brain gives the message to your whole body to get your whole system involved in the ordering process. This is important. One of the most amazing and powerful insights about the mind/body that Frank taught me is:

The mind *cannot tell the difference* between

a real and a vividly imagined experience.

What this means is that if you feed the mind a vividly imagined experience, the body accepts it as real. This is the basis of the Olympic Training Method where you train in your mind as much as you train on the actual course. You've seen athletes with their eyes closed moving their bodies as if going through the course before the race. They've not only trained hard physically, they've trained hard mentally. They've practiced seeing themselves doing the course perfectly. They've felt themselves making every maneuver of their sport. They've constantly fed their mind the information of how it's done perfectly. They've seen themselves wining and felt the elation of the gold medal around their neck. They've literally trained their bodies by training their minds

This concept of using the mind to train the physical body has also been applied to retraining the consciousness, or the psyche. It's called psycho-cybernetics. It was developed by the physician Dr. Maxwell Maltz, who reported the astonishing results of his work in the book <u>Psycho-Cybernetics</u>. It's a big word that simply means the goal-seeking behavior of the brain and nervous system. (Cybernetics is the Greek word for 'pilot'.) His book is dedicated to techniques that help you consciously change your self-images so you will then automatically make the changes you want in your life. Dr. Maltz used the brain's ability to create vivid self-images that the consciousness then accepts as reality.

Explained in terms of the chaos model, you change the outcome by choosing the ERI you put into your system. Practice the feelings (energetic patterns) that you want in your life. "Fake it 'til you make it" works with emotions. An interesting study that was done with actors proves this is true. Simply put, the study showed that while people were playing happy, energetic, optimistic roles, their bodies were measurably stronger, healthier, and more robust. When those same actors played roles that were angry, negative, depressed, hostile and pessimistic, their bodies were measurably weaker, more susceptible to disease. We can choose our feelings. The feelings we choose determine the energetic vibrations of our body. The law of attraction then determines what we draw into our life.

So, you ask Universe for what you want by feeling the feelings of already having it. Those feelings are the energetic order that you place with the Universal Fulfillment Center. Your vivid imagination literally helps program the energetic responses of Universe.

Simple steps to placing your order using affirming energy:

(1) Start your request with the words "I am. . ."

(2) Use the present tense. Action words end in –ing. "I am receiving x, y, z."

(3) Make your request positive. Avoid 'not' and negative descriptions.

(4) Keep it simple and brief.

(5) Use clear, specific words.

(6) Include vivid feeling words, like "enthusiastically", "joyfully", etc.

(7) Your request can only affect you. You can't do "Make my son behave!" You *can* do "I am creating a fun, understanding and loving relationship with my son." You can't create "John is falling in love with me." You *can* create, "I am confident because I am attracting exactly the kind of relationship I want."

Step # 4

4. *ASK. This seems obvious, but it's an important step that's often overlooked. You have to say the magic words: "I need help. Please help me with this."*

Asking is like placing the order in the mailbox. It's the final part of sending it out. The Universal Fulfillment Center can't fill an order that it doesn't have.

This part is really easy. You simply say. "I need help. Please help me with this." It's like sprinkling the fairy dust over your request that sends it on its way energetically. It announces to the quantum soup that you are open to input.

Step # 5

5. Stay Open. If you have programmed expectations about what the response will look like, you may overlook the answer to your order when it comes.

My favorite story that illustrates this is about George, a man of great faith. A flood came and George knew God would save him. George was on his roof and the waters were rising. His neighbor floated by on a door and held his hand out for George to climb on. George said, "No, God will save me." Then city workers came by in a rowboat and told George to get in. "No. I don't need to. God will save me." As the waters were engulfing his body, a Coast Guard helicopter lowered him a rope. He said "No. God will save me."

Water rises. George drowns. When George gets to the Gates, he's pretty miffed. He demands of St. Peter, "Why didn't God save me?" St. Peter just shook his head and said, "We tried three times." But George was so sure that he knew what God's saving him was going to look like that he missed the real thing. God's response didn't look like what he thought it should look like. You may spend your time looking for a stairway to drop from the clouds and miss a perfectly good door, boat or helicopter.

A quantum universe has millions of possibilities and will respond to you from its treasure. The response may not fit your expectations. But it will fill the need.

Step # 6

*6. Receive. When the solution
comes, claim it. Reach out and embrace
it. Take some action that confirms it as a
response you've asked for. If it's an idea
you receive that solves a problem,
verbally say "Bingo! Yes!" Shine the
spotlight of your acknowledgment on the
answer you've gotten.*

Quite often at this point I feel delighted. I'm
frequently amazed at the solutions of Divine
Oneness. And just as often, I'm entertained by how
humorous the response is.

Some time after Frank's death, the grieving
and life's responsibilities were weighing me down. I
was asking for more lightness in my life. One night
as I went to bed, I begged, "Please help me laugh."
When I awoke the next morning, I was smiling. Just
before waking up, Frank had appeared in my dream,
dressed as Picasso's tall skinny Don Quixote. It was
a very short cameo appearance. No story line.
Simply Frank standing there as Don Quixote. But
his kneecaps were layers of huge hubcaps . . . that
pulsed. They sprang way out, and then snapped
back. There was a twinkle in Don Frank's eyes as
he said, "Bet you can't do that with *your* kneecaps!"
I rolled out of bed and did high 5's with Universe.
That dream still makes me smile.

Remember that quantum reality includes the
dream world and other altered realities like
meditations, visions. Many scientists have gotten
solutions to their problems from these other
quantum realities. It was Einstein's ride on a light

beam that gave him the insight for his Theory of Relativity. Nicoli Tesla received the Tesla Coil in a very specific vision.

Receive your answers from wherever they come, and affirm that your request has been answered.

Step # 7

7. *Be grateful and celebrate!*
Imagine that you've taken the time and care to choose a unique gift for someone you love. You surprise them with this special something that is perfect for them. How would you feel if they take it and walk away? Chances are you wouldn't again take your time and effort to try to please them. But you'll want to keep them on your gift list if they show their delight and you feel their gratitude.

My experience with Divine Oneness is like that. Acknowledging the marvelous solutions of Universe seems to prime the pump for continual abundant responses.

While these seven steps may not be rules of the game, they are some of the protocol that seems to be honored by quantum reality.

At the core of quantum is co-creativity. We say, "This is Special Me. This is what I am. This is what I want." Quantum reality responds with "Great! Very cool expansion of the Whole you are! Will this help you? How about this? . . . or this? . . . or this??" Quantum reality responds to our assertion of our uniqueness by supplying the goods.

Universe continues to extend itself to us as partners in creation. As we enter in to the opportunity, we'll learn how to play.

Summary - Chapter 4

Uniqueness

I. **Amazing Grace**

A. The beginning: New Year's Day, the new millennium 2000

B. Story of move to Puerto Rico

C. When you're doing your unique work, things work out for your good.

D. Grace is the way the quantum world honors you when you are giving You.

II. Quantum Grace

A. Find and contribute your uniqueness – simply *be*

B. The way you *do* in the quantum world is to *be* . . . be the energetic vibration that will attract what you need.

C. Plant the Flag of 'You' as a verb.

D. Norma's wisdom: Our real work is discovering a bigger realm of who we are.

E. Your unique contribution strengthens the system and the system in return supports you:

    i. William Murray's Commitment quote;

    ii. The Internet as our first tool of energetic-uniqueness-marketing-matching. Put out your U.S.P. on the Web;

        iii. The realtor's sale despite being on
vacation.

    F. Be and allow (Don't push and do)

        i. Magic Eye;

        ii. Energetic attraction works on the
principle of allowing;

        iii. Pushing gets in the way of
allowing;

        iv. Peter Senge quote . . . If *doing* has
gotten us here, can *being* get us out?

III. Honey-Money (or How to *be*, productively)

    A. Bucky's precessional effect: your support
from Universe proceeds *indirectly*
from your work in the world.

    B. Bucky was a master at being his unique
self and allowing Universe to support
him: found what he could do that
wasn't being done.

    C. See Seiden's biography <u>Buckminster
Fuller's Universe: His Life and Work</u>.

    D. Bucky's fuller explanation in Appendix
A following this Summary.

    E. Star Trek video scene with Jean-Luc
Picard and Lily, "Titanium". What will
society look like when we have moved
beyond money as the direct
motivation?

IV. 7 Steps to Beeing

A. 1. Discover <u>Your Uniqueness</u>

B. 2. <u>Be You.</u>

C. 3. Get clarity on <u>What You Want</u>

D. 4. <u>Ask</u>

E. 5. Stay <u>Open</u>

F. 6. <u>Receive</u>

G. 7. <u>Celebrate</u> with <u>Gratitude</u>

Appendix A

Excerpt from

"Self-Disciplines of Buckminster Fuller"

A chapter in <u>Critical Path</u>

by R. Buckminster Fuller

The big question remained: How do you obtain the money to live with and to acquire the materials and tools with which to work?

The answer was "precession." What precession is, and why it was the answer, requires some explaining.

When we pull away from one another the opposite rigid-disk ends of a flexible, water-filled rubber cylinder, the middle part of the overall cylinder contracts in a concentric series of circular planes of diminishing radius perpendicular (at right angles) to the line of our pulling.

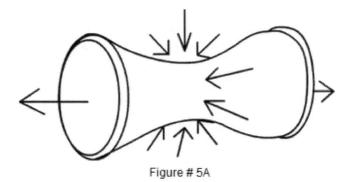

Figure # 5A

When we push toward one another on the two opposite ends of the same flexible, water-filled, rubber, rigid-disk-ended cylinder, the center of the cylinder swells maximally outward in a circular plane perpendicular (at right angles) to the line of our pushing together.

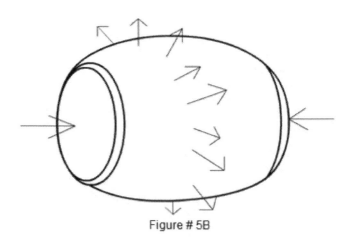

Figure # 5B

When we drop a stone in the water, a circular wave is generated that moves outwardly in a plane perpendicular (at right angles) to the line of stone-dropping — the outwardly expanding circular wave generates (at ninety degrees) a vertical wave that in turn generates an additional horizontally and outwardly expanding wave, and so on.

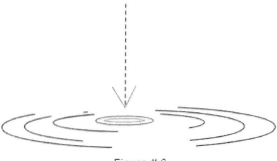

Figure # 6

All these right-angle effects are precessional effects. *Precession is the effect of bodies in motion on other bodies in motion.* The Sun and Earth are both in motion. Despite the 180-degree gravitational pull of the in-motion Sun upon the in-motion Earth, precession makes Earth orbit around the Sun in a direction that is at ninety degrees – i.e., at a right angle – to the direction of the Sun's gravitational pull upon Earth.

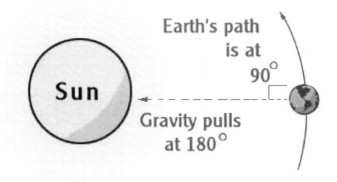

Figure # 7

The successful regeneration of life growth on our planet Earth is ecologically accomplished always and only as the precessional – right angled – "side effect" of the biological species' chromosomically programmed individual-survival preoccupations – the honeybees are chromosomically programmed to enter the flower blossoms in search of honey. Seemingly inadvertently (but realistically-precessionally) this occasions the bee's bumbling tail's becoming dusted with pollen (at ninety degrees to each bee's linear axis and flight path), whereafter the bee's further bumbling entries into other flowers inadvertently dusts off, pollenizes, and cross-fertilizes those flowers at right angles (precessionally) to the bee's operational axis – so, too, do all the mobile creatures of Earth cross-fertilize all the different rooted botanicals in one of another precessional (right-angled), inadvertent way.

Humans, as Honey-Money-seeking bees, do many of nature's required tasks only inadvertently.

They initially produce swords with metal-forging-developed capability, which capability is later used to make steel into farm plows. Humans – in politically organized, group-fear-mandated acquisition of weaponry – have inadvertently developed so-much-more-performance-with-so-much-less material, effort, and time investment per each technological task accomplished as now inadvertently to have established a level of technological capability which, if applied exclusively to peaceful purposes, can provide a sustainable high standard of living for all humanity, which accomplished fact makes war and all weaponry obsolete. Furthermore, all of this potential has happened only because of the at-ninety-degrees-realized generalized technology and science "side effects" or "fall-out" inadvertently discovered as special case manifest of the scientifically generalized principle of precession.

From Critical Path by R. Buckminster Fuller

REVIEW IN PICTURES
Chapters 1 and 2
(Energy and Systems)

> # LAW OF ENERGY
>
> It's all energy.
> Energy vibrates.
> Vibrations attract.

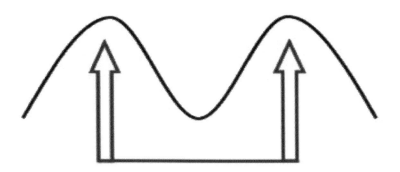

From arrow tip to arrow tip is one wave or cycle or frequency. Frequencies are measured in Hertz (Hz), or number of waves per second.

They can be high frequency with lots of waves per second, like this:

Or they can be low, with few cycles per second, like this:

The height of the wave is voltage. A wave

can have high voltage

Or it can have low voltage like this:

The power behind a wave is called
amperage. Waves can have lots of power
Behind them.

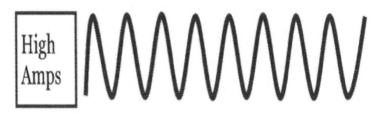

Or little power behind them.

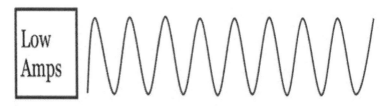

A wave's vibration can be smooth and regular:

Or it can be a spiky and irregular pattern:

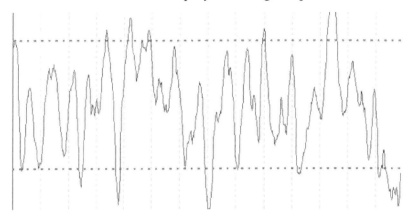

To keep it simple here (and with apologies to scientists) the combination of the speed, height, power, smoothness and regularity is called vibration. A vibration is the resulting pattern of all the variables. There are zillions of combinations of these functions. So there are literally an endless number of vibrations.

Everything (above the basic simple elements) has its own unique vibrational fingerprint. That energy fingerprint is created from the infinite combinations of limitless vibrations. So you are vibrationally unique. That's important to remember. It's the basis of fine tuning your magnetic attraction and broadcasting. It's also important in your ability to transform during chaos. (More on that later.)

Remember the ELM Spectrum at the beginning of Chapter 1? Remember the little slit of visible frequencies that make up what we see as light? At the top of the visible spectrum is violet. It vibrates the fastest. At the bottom of visible light is red which vibrates the slowest. If energy is vibrating faster than violet, we can't see it. If it's vibrating slower than red, we can't see it. The energy we can't see is called non-physical. It's real, just not visible to the eye.

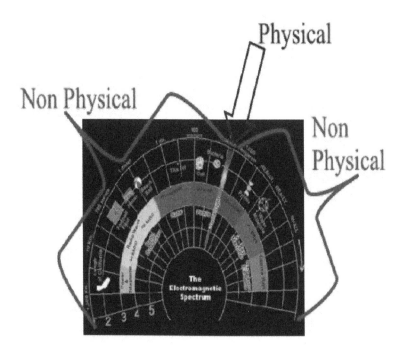

1 ~ Wavelength in meters
2 ~ Size of Wavelength
3 ~ Common name of wave
4 ~ Source of Wavelength
5 ~ Frequency (waves per second)

Just like with colors, physical objects have lower/slower vibrations and higher/faster vibrations.

A mold's vibrations are slower than a goldfish's which are slower than a human's.

Molds/viruses/bacteria/parasites *77 ~ 900 KHz (kilo-hertz)

Goldfish: 1000 KHz ~ 1300 KHz

Human *: 1520 KHz ~ 9460 KHz

* (Side note: This is how frequency health devices work. They use low voltage that is safe for humans and they send out frequencies (Hertz) that match the pathogens. This electronically 'zaps' and kills the pathogens without interfering with or harming the human body.)

Emotions have unique vibrations just like colors and physical objects do. These emotional vibrations also go from higher/faster to lower/slower. When you are laughing and having fun, your body's vibrations are lighter (higher and faster). When you are tired and sick your vibrations are heavier (slower and lower).

You know how when you are in love, you feel "energized", "high", like you're "walking on a cloud?" People say, "You're 'glowing'." That's because your emotions are literally adding voltage and power, lightening your body. And when you're negative and depressed, you feel sluggish, "low," "heavy". "I'm down today." Your emotional vibrations are giving your body a slower, lower vibration. This is not speaking metaphorically. This

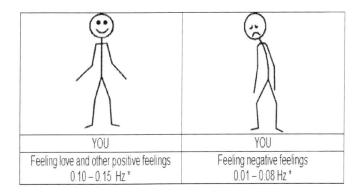

YOU	YOU
Feeling love and other positive feelings 0.10 – 0.15 Hz *	Feeling negative feelings 0.01 – 0.08 Hz *

is scientifically measurable. (<u>Molecules of Emotion</u> by Dr. Candace Pert, and HeartMathInstitute.),

Entrainment frequencies in Hz. above are as measured on

Power Spectrum Graph, Heart Math Institute research

For those of you who are math-challenged, these measurements mean that when we feel love we vibrate at a higher frequency. When we feel negative feelings we vibrate at a lower frequency. In addition to measuring them, we can also take pictures of these emotional vibrations. Kirlian photography shows our energy field and the effect our emotions have on our bodies.

We can take these pictures and measure our body's frequencies because human beings are electromagnetic (ELM) energy. And our ELM energy vibrates or pulses. With every pulse, your ELM energy both broadcasts out and attracts in. Your energy field transmits your vibrations and magnetizes other similar vibrations into your energy

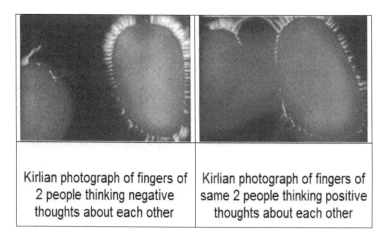

| Kirlian photograph of fingers of 2 people thinking negative thoughts about each other | Kirlian photograph of fingers of same 2 people thinking positive thoughts about each other |

field. You are constantly broadcasting your own
energy and attracting other energy.

We humans are like a satellite dish that can
send and receive at the same time.

YOU as a satellite *broadcasting* your
intentions (in a moving flow, top left to right) and

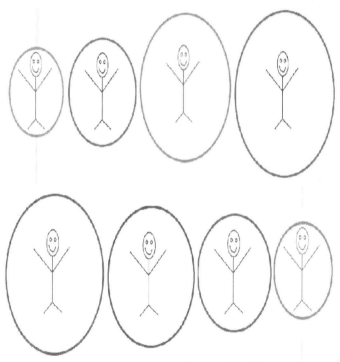

attracting to you what you've focused on
(bottom left to right)

Like a satellite dish, the direction you turn
determines what comes into the dish of your energy
field. What you attract into your field is your
energetic food. It is literally what you are feeding
yourself. Again, this is not speaking metaphorically.

This is scientifically measurable in the good ol'
Newtonian way.

The phrase 'garbage in, garbage out' takes
on new meaning. Understanding this gives us clear
choices if we want to choose health and well-being.
Remember "Choice counts. Always." The choice of
where you look shapes you. You are choosing the
make-up of your body by what you digest
energetically just like what you eat by mouth affects
your body.

Simple choices, profound results. Do you
choose to focus:

On the trash in the gutter, or the
blossoms on the trees?

On the criticism of Funky Francis, or on the cooperation offered by Creative Kim?

On pain and suffering, or on health and happiness?

While trash is visible to us in the ELM, criticism and failures are non-physical vibrational realities that are absorbed by our body. They are just as real as the physical food eaten by mouth. Negative emotions pollute our body just like junk food. Positive emotions nurture our body just like gourmet health food.

When you absorb a frequency into your energetic body over along period of time, it permanently contributes its resonance to you. Remember how magnets are made? A constant intake of a certain frequency literally magnetizes your body to that frequency.

REVIEW IN PICTURES
Chapters 3 and 4
(Chaos and Uniqueness)

This is what a system in chaos looks like at explosion point from an energy perspective. Remember from Chapter 3 and the Kirk Model of Chaos that there are **Stability-seeking (S)** parts and **Balance Far From Equilibrium-seeking (B)** parts. (And remember that 'part' really means 'sub-system'.)

The Stability-seeking units are non-communicating, rigid, angular, brittle, thick, non-porous, tight, etc. They have little energy because they are closest to entropy/death. They have low/no vibration.

The Balance-seeking units are brushing up against each other and communicating, flexible, responsive, etc. They are vibrating a lot because they have more energy.

Think of this model as You in Chaos. This is your emotional body at the point of explosion. You have both **S** parts and **B** parts.

Ready? Go!

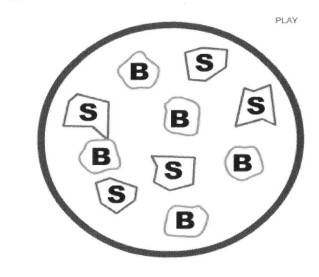

PLAY

You in Chaos
At Explosion Point

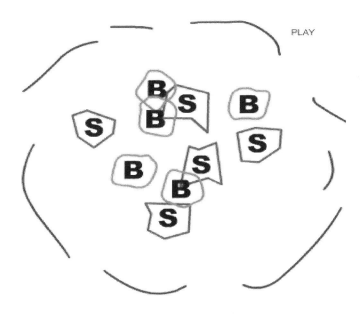

PLAY

As your tolerance boundaries snap,

your jumbled mess of emotions fly apart . . .

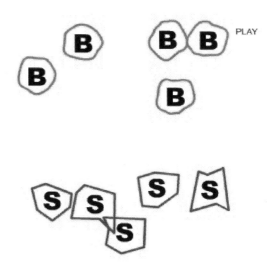

. . . and reassemble, like attracted to like.

Which raw material will your system now use?

The energy you feed your system determines the vibrational resilience at the explosion point. If you feed a human system blame, shame, criticism, ugliness, anger, hate, violence, you get a system that is fearful, closed, withdrawn, rigid, weak. That brittleness translates to disintegration at explosion point.

If you feed the system encouragement, delight, joy, playfulness, you get a Balance-seeking system that is fluid, open, responsive, flexible . . . that at explosions point can transform, reform to a higher vibration, more complex, more capable of handling more new information (ERI.) It now has higher capacity. The deadwood (lower vibrating stuff) that was slowing it down is gone. The new form is made up of higher frequency stuff that is more fluid and receptive. It can expand and take in more energy without exploding.

The clearer you are about your uniqueness, who you are (and aren't), the stronger your vibrational message is and the better your chances are of finding (being vibrationally attracted to) similar people/systems (like-minded, like-spirited)

> ## LAW OF ENERGY
>
> # Uniqueness strengthens systems

after explosions.

There is new research in the Unified Field Theory arena. (That's the one that gave Einstein his pulling-the-hair-out-of-my-head coif in his later years.) The new research says, and allegedly proves, that the unifying force is . . . (drum roll. . . . . . Ta-dah!!!!!!!) *Consciousness.* This will be explored in Chapter 5 along with the question "What creates a quantum event?"

Chapter 5
The Quantum Event

The Quantum Milkman

It's the summer of 1985. I'm being driven through the countryside south of Mogadishu, Somalia. Somalia is a land of nomadic people on the horn of East Africa. It is the birthplace of the young woman Arda who has been living with Tom and me in Denver for over a year now. She's learning English and The American Way in preparation for college.

At the wheel on this summer afternoon is Abdi Mohamud Kheyre, Arda's father. Reserved, handsome, intelligent Abdi. He proudly tells me about his homeland as we drive. Today he has taken us to the beach at Merca, for a lobster lunch in a little park restaurant, and for a stop at a town market in Afgooye. He stops the car to let a herd of goats cross the road. A few miles back, it was for 2 tall slender Somalis with their spears and camels.

Sitting next to Abdi in the front seat is Arda's mother Hawa Hassan. She's a stately woman dressed in her colorful Somali 'dirac' robes. A similar bright 'shaash' is draped over her head according to Somali custom for a married woman. Hawa is laughing and talking, her smile flashing out often. She's wearing an abundance of Arabic gold for the occasion. In Somalia, being skinny is a sign of poverty. So Hawa's size is a tribute to her husband's wealth and standing in the community.

In the back seat, Arda is translating the proceedings for me. Farxiya, Hodan and Zem-Zem, 3 of her younger sisters entertain themselves or gaze out the window. Suddenly, one of them yells, "Nirig! Nirig!" I don't need Arda to translate as I look out and see Baby Camel nursing under its mother.

I'm hopping up and down with excitement as Abdi pulls the car over. I get to see Baby Camel . . . up close and personal! The camels are some distance off the road to the left of us. Baby Camel looks like a cross between a teddy bear and a baby deer with its long wobbly legs and its fuzzy caramel-colored coat.

The little girls have charged ahead, with Hawa leading Arda and me bringing up the rear of the parade. Abdi decides to stay in the car for a well-earned catnap. Mother Camel is tied to a tree. Baby Camel is now huddled behind its mother, its meal interrupted by our explosion into its quiet afternoon.

I am within fifty feet of the camels when a shout and sudden movement from the right stops me short. I turn to see an angry bare-chested Somali nomad with a spear in his hand headed for me. I freeze. I see that he has come out of a hut that I wasn't even aware was there. I am obviously in someone's front yard and he's mad. I had a terrible sinking feeling in the pit of my stomach. (I knew that many Somalis had a well-founded hatred of foreigners.)

The little girls had huddled behind Hawa. By her utter silence, I knew she was as shocked as I was. Hawa started talking quietly, making her way towards me. His hostility only increased. The combination of rich, big-city Somali woman and foreigner just intensified his anger. He's shaking his spear now.

Then Hawa stopped in midstream. Her head went forward as she peered at him. Then she burst out laughing. "Ahmed! Ahmed! Hawa! Hawa Hassan!" He looked startled. "Hawa? Hawa Dhanane?!!" Then I saw the look of recognition in his eyes and watched it spread to his body. He lowered his spear. His whole demeanor softened. He smiled and laughed. He and Hawa hugged in the traditional warm Somali greeting. Just like old friends, which is what they were. Turns out that Ahmed had delivered fresh camel milk to Hawa for years when they lived in their old home in another part of Mogadishu.

So here we were. Standing in the front yard of Hawa's milkman. Ahmed glowed as Hawa bragged that he had the best camel milk around. And of course, being the best camel milkman around, Ahmed generously offered us all a drink of fresh warm camel milk. Arda warned me that it's better when it's aged a little . . . kind of like buttermilk. But I was just getting my knees back and was grateful for Ahmed's gesture of kindness. I was more than willing to swallow a little weird tasting camel milk, silently thanking whatever had placed us in the yard of Hawa's milkman.

Ahmed and Hawa chatted. Hawa the socialite filled in the country milkman on their friends in the old neighborhood. I really wanted to cuddle Baby Camel, but under the circumstances, I was satisfied to just edge my way closer, squat and smile at it. Baby Camel didn't look like it wanted to be petted anyway.

Pretty soon, we all thanked Ahmed and made our way back to the car. We woke Abdi who had missed the whole drama. As the little ones were getting in, I looked back. The scene was once again tranquil. The only difference was that now I saw a bigger picture. Mother and Baby Camel were part of a little homestead that included Ahmed's hut.

I remember that I wanted to *see* the energy of what had just happened. I wanted a Slow Motion Energy Camera to show me the love-fear-love cycle. I wanted to see what the energy of delight looks like when it's attacked by fear and turns to fear. What does fear look like when confronted with overwhelming, unfrightened love? What does the energy of fear look like as it dissolves into laughter?

I'll never forget how fast things changed when Hawa recognized Ahmed. And when Ahmed suddenly realized that the enemy was an old friend.

Arda's family in the garden of their
Mogadishu home, 1985.

Left to right standing: Deeqa, Sahara, Arda

Seated: Ayan (Zem-Zem), Abdi, Farxiya
(kneeling), Mohamed (on Hawa's chair),

Hodan (on Hawa's lap), Hawa

The Energy of a Human Quantum Event

I can now understand the energy of that event. We don't yet have the slow motion energy camera that I want. But I'm sure we'll have one within a few dozen decades (to borrow a Jean Houston phrase). Quantum and chaos have explained the energy dynamics to me. To me, it looks like this.

My delighted energy. "I get to see Baby Camel."

My joy gives me a happy frequency: high, fast, smooth.

Love is my main vibration.

NEXT FRAME

Ahmed's anger is stronger than my delight and brings my fear to the surface. Ahmed's fear (anger is always fear of losing something) is intense. It's the strongest pendulum going at that point. It's more powerful than my delight which gets pushed down as Ahmed's fear entrains/magnetizes my fear frequencies to the surface.

Fear is now my main vibration.

NEXT FRAME

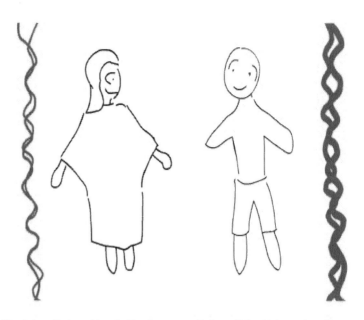

Hawa's deep affection and love for Ahmed overpowers his fear and brings his love to the surface.

Her strong love entrains his love.

Love is now his main vibration.

The emotions of this model are simplified. The two most basic emotions are love and fear. (Some say there is only love and the absence of love.) For the purposes of this chapter, emotional energy is simplified. It's all variations on the theme of either love or fear. Seen in this light, the energy in the Somali scene snapped from love to fear, and back to love.

How would quantum physics explain this non-physical energy event? Where does Ahmed's fear vibration go? It is energy, so it doesn't disappear or evaporate. (Remember First Law of Thermodynamics: Energy is neither created nor destroyed, only changed.) Is it dissolved and dissipated out of the system of Ahmed? Or is it simply overwhelmed and pushed into a minor vibrational status within the system? Where did my love go when I absorbed Ahmed's fear? Did it leave my system? Or did it get overpowered and become a minor vibration? Can we learn to increase love energy and decrease fear energy – permanently? Can we learn to hold love energy in the face of the strongest fear? How? And when equal power (amperages) of love vibration and fear vibration are face to face with each other, what happens?

And what do the energetic frequencies of love and fear have to do with quantum, anyway?

To answer that, I went back to the beginning: The definition of quantum and what makes a quantum event.

Quantum comes from 'quantity'. A quanta is a quantity, an amount. It is a unit of measurement. It is the smallest amount of energy that can exist independently, and that can move independently.

A very strange thing about quanta is *how* it moves. It does not travel through the space in between the two spots. It leaps, instantaneously. Now you see it. Now you don't. It's here. Then it's there. And there's no halfway point.

In Newtonian Physics, we can watch X move as it goes from point A to point B. But in quantum, X goes from point A to point B without covering the ground in between. A quantum event at the sub-atomic level is a 'Beam me up, Scottie' type of travel.

In terms of the chaos cycle, what happens at the explosion point can be seen as a quantum non-linear event. One moment the system is in maximum chaos. The next moment the system is in order. One moment you're in total turmoil. The next moment you're in calm. At the explosion point, all the tension releases and suddenly . . . you've moved miles (or light-years) from where you were. Your system's relationship to the issue/new information that was upsetting it has snapped. The anxiety is gone – replaced by a new way of seeing the issue or even a total disinterest in it. The problem isn't a problem anymore. The system has leaped beyond the issue. The issue itself rarely changes. It's still there. But the system has changed and the old issue just doesn't cause you any grief now.

And you're not aware of how you got here. Can you turn around and retrace the steps? Can you cover the ground between where you were at explosion point and where you are now? You've gone from point A to point B without traveling through the distance in between. You have simply arrived. The non-linear pop.

Energetically speaking, change can happen in a Newtonian way or in a quantum way. Newtonian change can be tracked. You see the cause and effect. The cycle itself (of chaos-order-chaos-order) is a Newtonian cycle. We can predict that an orderly living system left alone will go into chaos. And we can predict that an uninterrupted living system in chaos will find its way to order. The cycle itself is predictable. In fact, it's not really Chaos Theory. It's Order Theory. It's about chaos that always resolves into order, if left to its natural process. If we can see the chaotic picture big enough, there's always order there.

So the chaos cycle itself is Newtonianly predictable. However, *within the Newtonian cycle is the quantum event*: the unpredictable that happens at the explosion point. The system takes a non-linear jump and arrives somewhere else without covering the ground in between.

At the explosion point the system either scatters energy and falls apart, or refines energy and reforms. In transformation, it comes together in a way that can incorporate more energy.

Every time you transform, you

1. drop deadwood

2. use energy

3. add complexity

Every time you disintegrate, you

1. keep deadwood

2. waste energy

3. lose complexity

Transformation is a jump to a higher vibration. As separate things come together and bond as a new system, new energy is added to the system. The system now contains more and higher frequencies than before.

Disintegration is the drop to a simpler energetic state with fewer and lower frequencies. The units of the system have splintered and disconnected from each other. They've lost their bond and scattered apart. Disintegration is a move towards isolation and separation, towards a more simplified form with fewer options.

A Wrinkle in Time

How does it help to know this: that it is within the Newtonian process that the quantum leap event happens at the explosion point? The key question still is: Is there anything we can do to hedge our bets in favor of transformation instead of disintegration? Can I better answer that question by knowing that the quantum event happens inside the Newtonian process?

Remember from Chapter 3: it is the choices we make during the cooking time that set the history of the organism. That history is the energetic pattern that can determine the outcome after explosion. It is that pattern, that web of strong energy that can draw the scattered pieces back together to form the new more complex system . . . or the lack of a strong energetic pattern that allows the system to disintegrate.

That energetic pattern is the system's *memory.* A memory is a *web of energy*, non-physical and real. When the frequencies of the energy web are strong, it can attract new matter to it as well as the old pieces of matter that still resonate with it. This is why the newly formed system has more energy and is more complex. It has attracted to it new matter that matches its vibration. This makes a physical system similar to the former system that scattered at the explosion point. Except it's better, energetically speaking.

This is a model of the memory cycle, showing both the physical matter and non-physical energetic parts of the cycle.

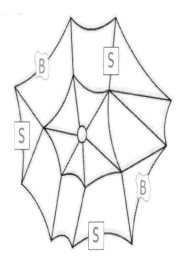

Memory History: the energy web (black) with physical matter (yellow) attached to it. See that there are both S (Stability-seeking) and B (Balance-seeking) pieces on the energy web.

B Balance

S Stability

The energetic web of memory is formed during the cooking time. (Remember that the cooking time is how you react when the ERI comes into your system and disturbs it.) The energetic web has attracted and solidified matter to it, so it has material substance. The matter attached to it can be everything from the body's toxins to a muscular usage pattern. The belief patterns have become physical. They are now attached to the energetic web. For example, the belief that "I'm sick and weak and I can't handle this disturbance" becomes a chunk of S toxins that hook onto the energetic web, making it rigid. The belief "I'm basically strong and resilient and I can handle this emergency" becomes a piece of B endorphin-like matter that attaches to the memory's energetic web, making it stronger.

NEXT FRAME

At the explosion point the physical matter is scattered.

It is denser, so the shock wave of the explosion knocks it off and scatters it.

NEXT FRAME

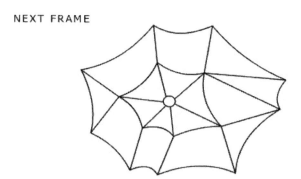

The energetic non-physical pattern remains. This is the system's memory.

The system's memory is an energetic web

This energetic memory attracts new substance to it. The vibrating energy web acts like a magnet. It attracts both some of the old and some new energy to it. It will attract back to itself pieces of the former system that are still vibrating the same as it. It will also attract new pieces that are vibrating the same as it. In this way, the new system is bigger and better. It has more energy and is more cohesive.

The new system that forms
around the memory
is higher and more complex,
able to handle increased ERI.

An example of this memory energy cycle is on your own skin. Think of a wrinkle you have. If you don't have a wrinkle (wow ☺), think of a mole or scar. Any skin blemish will do. What keeps that wrinkle in your skin? It's not your skin cells. They die and are replaced every 30 days. Every month you get fresh new skin cells on that skin blemish. So if I have new skin, why do I have an old wrinkle? (Other than to fund the billion dollar cosmetics industry, that is.)

Why do I keep the wrinkle? I keep the wrinkle because of my skin's memory. There is an energetic web of memory that draws the new cells into the old form. New cells in the old wrinkle. Darn!

The cycle looks like this: This is a wrinkle (greatly enlarged). As seen from the side, it looks like the Grand Canyon.

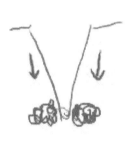

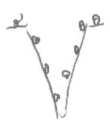

Phase I:
Wrinkle made of
millions of skin cells

Phase II:
Cells dying and
sluffing (sloughing) off.
This leaves the
energetic memory pattern.

Phase III:
Fresh new cells
coming in attaching
to the old memory.
(Shucks!)

The energetic memory pattern is especially important after the explosion point. If it's strong enough, it creates the field that attracts parts back to it to form a new system. When it's strong enough, the system trans-forms. It takes on a new form at a higher more complex level.

An energetic memory pattern is a belief. A belief is formed when you repeatedly accept something as true. Repeatedly doing something or believing something makes it into an energetic memory. That energetic memory then locks the system's body into a reality based on that belief. "Seeing is believing" has it backwards. It's actually "Believing is seeing." When you believe something, that is what you will see. Your energetic belief is attracting what you then see as reality. Sad but true: It is our belief that we are aging that attracts the wrinkles that then confirm that. Have you ever seen an old person who ought to have wrinkles and gray hair but doesn't? (And not because they've been surgically sucked, tucked and tinted.) Keep your eyes open. They're rare, but they're out there.

Since our mind creates the pattern, can we undo the pattern the same way? By believing something different? Of course. But how?

Change Beliefs &
Change the System's History

The brain has a nifty device. It's called the Reticular Activation System, or RAS for short. It's our belief-maker and our belief-breaker. It can help us change beliefs. Beliefs create actions which create history.

Beliefs → Actions → History

So when we change our beliefs, we change our history. By changing our history, we may hedge our bets in favor of transformation at explosion point.

The way the RAS works is simple. It screens all the information coming in to the brain. Our five senses give us thousands of bits of information every second. This much input would overwhelm us, so the brain screens most of it out. Less than 1% of this sensate information actually gets through to our consciousness. Good system. But what decides which information gets through?

The RAS lets through *only that information which agrees with our beliefs.* The information that does not match our beliefs doesn't make the cut. For example, have you ever bought a new car? You've looked around, compared, and narrowed it to 2 kinds of cars: a Ford Mustang and a Toyota Prius. You decide on the Prius and you buy it. Now, you start noticing Prius everywhere. This is not because there are suddenly more Prius in the world. It's because you have decided that Prius is a good car. You've reprogrammed your brain and *opened your RAS* to Prius. Your RAS will now let through all the Prius in your environment.

Paradigm is another word for a pattern of belief. Joel Barker is well known for his groundbreaking work with paradigms. His corporate training videos and books are excellent. (*starthrower.com, The New Business of Paradigms,* <u>Five Regions of the Future</u>) His research shows just how strong the effect of the RAS is. His work is further proof that only that material that agrees with what we already think gets through. Said differently, we literally do not see, hear or receive information that does not agree with our beliefs. If I believe the earth is flat, I will not receive any information to the contrary. If I believe Republicans are good and Democrats are bad, my RAS will only admit information that supports that. If I hate Christians (or Muslims or Jews), then my RAS will only give me facts that justify my hatred. If I believe the world is a frightening violent place, that's the information I will continue to get . . . unless I reprogram my RAS.

This is a model of how your RAS works. It acts like a funnel. All sensate information (sight, sound, taste, touch, smell) comes into the funnel. It goes down the side in little chunks. The RAS robot sits by your library of programs. When it sees a chunk of information coming that's about men, for example, it finds your program on "Men". It plugs it into your RAS computer. The trap door opens. Everything that is contrary to what you believe about men drops through the trap door into the depths of your unconscious. Only the part that agrees with what you already believe about men will get through to your consciousness.

Specifically, it looks like this. It's Monday morning after Mother's Day. You are on break with your female colleagues. Sarah says, "Juan did the sweetest thing for me yesterday. . ." Ramita says, "You know, I just can't figure out how a husband of 15 years thinks a toaster is a great Mother's Day

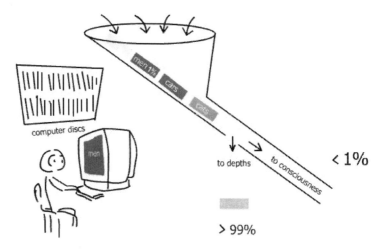

The RAS supports your beliefs

gift!" If you believe that men are thoughtful and caring, you'll hear Sarah's comment, take it up and add your own. If you believe that men are inconsiderate jerks, who are you going to hear? Your ears pick up the sounds of the entire conversation. But your brain will register only the part that agrees with your program. Unless you reprogram your RAS.

Reprogramming the RAS is simple. That's the good news. You simply make the decision to let in new information, and tell your RAS to open up to something new. . . and really mean it. (I said simple. I didn't say easy.) For example, if you're a woman who thinks men are jerks, you tell yourself that you want to change how you feel about men. You tell your RAS that you want to get a balanced objective view of men. You tell it to let through ALL the information about men. If you're a Christian who fears Muslims, you tell yourself you want to get to know some friendly Muslims and learn about Islam. If you've always been a Democrat, tell your RAS you want to open up to receive the valuable views of Republicans. If you had an alcoholic father and hate being around people who drink, tell your RAS that you want to learn to be comfortable around people who are responsible drinkers. If you really mean it, the RAS will do the rest. And you're on your way to creating a new history for yourself which will give you new results when the next crisis/chaos jolts into your life.

In order to experience something different, you have to choose to open up to a new way of seeing, to a different reality. This different reality may convince you that your previous reality no longer serves you, even though it did serve you until now. Remember nature's question: Does it benefit the system?

If you decide that a new reality works better for you now, then you have to create a new memory for your cells to form around. You do that by making choices consistent with the reality you want until it becomes a pattern. The new pattern must become stronger than the old pattern before the old pattern dies. Technically it doesn't die since energy is never destroyed. The new pattern simply overpowers the old pattern. The old one weakens due to starvation because you're not feeding it any new energy.

GUT-TOE Answer?

There's an exciting new theory in the quest for the Unified Field. Briefly, the Unified Field Theory (or the GUT, the Grand Unified Theory; or TOE Theory Of Everything) is the search for the missing energetic link. Science has believed that there are only 4 forces. They are:

1.gravity

2.ELM or electromagnetism

3.weak nuclear force

4.strong nuclear force

No one to date has been able to explain the energetic link that ties them all together. Including Einstein. He spent his later years tearing his hair out in search of the unified theory.

I've been mildly intrigued with the search for The Unified Theory for years. I remember when I was moving into my Puerto Rican house in December, 2000. Becky and I had a most interesting conversation about a scientist she'd just spent some time with in California who said he'd proven that the unifying force was (TA! DAH!) *Consciousness.* I remember the explosion going off in my head when Becky said, "consciousness." I remember thinking, "BAM! That's it! Of course. Makes perfect sense. How else could these wildly different forces become coherent with each other, except through consciousness?"

I have searched for a definition of consciousness. The best one I've found (my own) is:

Consciousness

is the

awareness

of connection to the whole

For example, healthy cells are conscious because they communicate with the whole body and know their function within that whole. Cancer cells aren't conscious because they don't know their connection to the whole. They have walled themselves off into a false community, the proliferation of which kills the host. A person who litters is unconscious because they are fowling their own nest. They don't understand their connection to the whole community. And a person who has been knocked unconscious with a blow to the head is unaware of their connection to their body and their physical surroundings.

Conscious Choice or

Unconscious Reaction?

What does it mean to make a conscious choice, in terms of a living system? What does it mean to unconsciously react?

A little scenario came my way that helped me clarify this. It was early on a quiet Saturday morning. I was walking to the back yard of my new beautiful home in Rincon, Puerto Rico to pick some Hibiscus flowers for the day. As I passed the cabana, I saw that the bike was gone, so Megan, who rented the cabana, had already left for work. Then I noticed that the refrigerator and freezer doors were open. Odd. That's not like Megan. I went in to close them . . . and went into shock. The cabana had been ransacked. Clothes were thrown everywhere. Drawers were pulled open. The closets were open. All the kitchen cabinets were open, and food and dishes had been moved to the desk.

I stood in the middle of the cabana, breathing. "OK, calm down. No one's been hurt. There's no blood. There's no violence. Nothing's been broken or smashed. Nothing's permanently ruined." As I got calmer, I noticed more. Nothing had been taken. The CD player was there. No damage to the computer. I didn't feel like whoever was here had been angry and violent, or intent on destruction. If they weren't stealing things, were they just after money? Had they taken anything from Megan?

It was a very creepy feeling to know that someone had simply walked into my cabana in broad daylight and wreaked havoc. I felt scared and invaded and defenseless and mad.

I got in the car to go tell Megan. I wanted to tell her in person rather than on the phone. Also I realized I was shook up, and I really wanted to be with a friend. As I was driving I asked myself, "Why am I scared? What am I afraid of?" It boiled down to 2 things: First, I was afraid that this would happen again. That this was an indicator of 'increasing violence'. I'd have to call the police -- deal with an investigation in my bad Spanish or their broken English. I was afraid now that someone had broken in, some undesirable elements would think that I was an easy target, etc. Bottom line, that I would have to do something to increase my protection: get guard dogs, put in a security system, put locks on the gates, build a wall around the yard, etc.

Secondly, I was afraid that Megan would feel scared and move out . . . that I would lose her as a friend and renter. I pulled up to the garden at the Ann Wigmore Natural Health Institute where

Megan was working. I decided that in addition to telling her what had happened, I also needed to tell her I was afraid she'd want to move. It's my way of facing fear: put it in words.

Megan is one in a million. When I told her that her apartment had just been ransacked, she was totally calm. She said, "You know, about ten minutes ago, I was working with the soil. I was on my knees, running the rich compost through my fingers, and I was thinking, 'The most important thing to me in the world is this earth. Nothing matters more to me than this.'" She didn't even say, "I wonder if they took my money." I had to ask her if she'd had any cash anywhere. (When I got back to the cabana, her money was still there.) When I told her I was afraid she'd move, she laughed and said, "I like it there. Why would I move?"

I called my local friend Charlie to talk over whether I should call the police. (And for comfort. I was still feeling alone and vulnerable.) Charlie told me that his son's shop, the Taino Divers, had recently been hit in the same way: nothing taken or broken, just thrown around. The police said it was a local crazy woman. "She's harmless. She just wanders into places and liberates whatever's in drawers, cabinets, refrigerators. Doesn't like to see things closed in."

I cleaned up the cabana and called Luis to come put a lock on it.

When I'm in chaos, it helps me to think in terms of conscious choice instead of unconscious reaction. The difference looks like this.

Unconscious Reaction:

~ <u>fear-based</u>: I'm in trouble.

~ <u>knee-jerk response</u>: Call the police.

~ <u>it's about security</u>: I've got to protect myself.

~ <u>small system approach</u>: They're after me.

~ <u>blame</u>: Find the offender and punish them.

Conscious Choice:

~ <u>trust-based</u>: I'm OK.

~ <u>thoughtful observation</u>: What are the facts? (objective, unemotional)

~ <u>it's about information</u>: There's a message here. What is it?

~ <u>big system picture</u>: What's happening in the larger system?

~ <u>responsibility</u>: What's my part of the problem that I can fix?

(Like, how about putting a lock on the door, Phyllis.)

Think of a problem you have had recently. What was the problem? What would have been an unconscious reaction to the problem? What would have been a conscious response? What is a problem you have now? What is an unconscious reaction to it? What does a conscious choice look like?

Every decision is an option between an unconscious reaction and a conscious response. As we become aware of our unconscious patterns, we can change how they affect our life.

Strange Attractor

There's one other weird quantum concept that helps us understand chaos. It has been given a scientific name that I love: Strange Attractor. Here's how I explained its usefulness in an article I wrote for *Vision* magazine.

The Strangely Attracting Self
In Chocolate Wonderland

ASSIGNMENT:

Study of the Social Structure of Earth nation called United States of America (Star Date <-4> 83930.41) Does this nation's social infrastructure support and enhance development of individual human (individualization)?

REPORT:

A most interesting region of Solar-bound humans, this United States. We find a diverse array of technology, arts, and institutions. There is advanced informational equipment that is individual-connecting, people-centered and user-driven.

This nation segregates its wisdom generation as 'old' and removes many of them to holding ghettos called 'nurse houses'. Yet they lead other Earth cultures in honoring their environment in awareness they call 'ecology'.

They are the richest nation on the planet. They are also the sickest and the most violent measured by the percent of their national economy that goes toward medical and war institutions.

Most interesting is this: They are ahead of other Earth cultures in what we call expansive individuating opportunities.

We recommend continued monitoring for potentially meaningful contributions.

SUBMITTED BY:

Spock, Jr. Science Officer, U.S.S.Enterprise (NCC-1701)

If Mr. Spock interviewed you, how would you answer him? Do the US's social structures enhance meaningful lives for individuals? Does the self prosper here in this living system we call the United States?

Bhutan is a small Himalayan country that gives priority to happiness as a political goal. Bhutan believes that true social advancement only takes place if material and spiritual development occur together. Gross National Happiness, GNH, is a guiding principle in all policies and plans.

If I were born in Bhutan, would my self have a better shot at happiness? Am I in a sense handicapped by being born in the US? If my goal is happiness, is it a disadvantage to be bathed in choice, abundance, technology and glitz? The self within the social structure is similar to a loom. The vertical strands anchored to the loom at the top and bottom are like society's framework. They represent the 'givens' that we have in our lives: national economy, quality of education and health care, time and place we're born, censorship/freedom of information, etc. The loom's handheld shuttle that weaves the horizontal thread across the vertical strands represents the individual within the social structure. The threads that the shuttle-self selects are the 'chosens' in life.

The vertical threads, the social framework, do not determine the outcome. They only support the final creation on my loom. They could be gold filaments of a good education, stretchy rubber bands of a dysfunctional childhood, or the plastic fishing line of a depression. They are just fixed strands that I move through as I weave my chosen horizontal threads. I decide which of the vertical threads I want to engage and which ones I pass over so they don't show on the front of the final piece. And I decide what I use as my fiber to go through the vertical givens. I can weave with soiled and tangled yarn of anger, pessimism and worry. Or I can choose colorful fabric ribbons of passion, gratitude, trust and forgiveness. Both the vertical givens and the horizontal chosens create the final tapestry that comes from my loom of life.

The self can flourish in the worst social conditions. Wangari Maathai, an East African woman who's been beaten and repeatedly arrested for her empowerment politics, is an example. She became a Nobel Peace Prize winner for her Green Belt Movement focused on planting trees across Africa and maintaining open green space in cities where developers wanted buildings. Victor Frankl wrote Man's Search for Meaning after surviving years of brutal dehumanization in Nazi concentration camps.

The real question for the self is: What emotions and experiences do I want in my life, and how do I get them? Enter: The Strange Attractor.

In quantum physics, the strange attractor is an invisible point that makes random arrows of energy return to it repeatedly. A strange attractor creates patterns out of the chaos. In that way, it's sort of like the outer layer of the brain, the neo-cortex, which seeks to make meaning out of a mass of random data. A strange attractor shapes things into patterns based on the formula programmed into its core.

This is one of the most famous, called the Lorenz Strange Attractor. It self-generated on the computer when Edward Lorenz was developing a math model for atmospheric convection (wind and storms). What a coincidence that it looks like a butterfly.

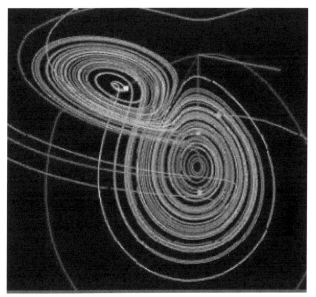

Lorenz Strange Attractor

The strange attractor is a stable constant in the whirling changes. The self is the strange attractor in the social structure that gives the soul meaning. As you accept the reality of it and pay attention to how it works, your strange attractor can be one of your self's strongest allies.

I used to be a news junkie. I read local and international dailies, and constantly listened to news. When I went to live in Moscow in 1989, the Iron Curtain was still very much up. Life for Westerners in Moscow at that time was almost as isolated from the outside world as it was for Soviets. International mail, newspapers and phone service was somewhere between impossible and non-existent. I got through my news addiction withdrawal and got used to life without it.

When I returned from Moscow, I lived by choice in a home that was TV and newspaper-free. I began to understand Mass Consciousness . . . or perhaps it's Mass Unconsciouness. What I realized was: first, that the news I had thought was critical to my life, wasn't; and second, what I needed to know came to me in interesting and unpredictable ways. Somehow, I was getting exactly what was valuable and important for me.

The most significant example of this happened in 2005 when I was living in San Diego. At a stoplight with a bus on my left, I glanced up and saw a TV in the bus. Scrolling across the monitor was former President Clinton's quote honoring Rosa Parks. That is how I found out she had just died. Rosa had lit the candle of the Civil Rights Movement in the US and she was a heroine of mine. I was touched by her life. Something knew that I would want to know about Rosa's death, and it gave me that special moment.

I accept a scientific explanation that goes something like this: My longtime interest in Rosa Parks created a Rosa Parks frequency in me. My Rosa parks frequency is continually active whether I am thinking about her or not. That Rosa frequency attracts Rosa information to me from my environment whenever and wherever it is.

Rosa Parks in 1955. Her refusal to give up her seat to a white passenger

on the bus started the 11 month Montgomery Bus Boycott.

Notice Dr. Martin Luther King in the background.

Months later, I realized that the Whatever had given me the news about Rosa Parks from the inside of a *bus* as I was sitting next to it. I still smile at that one.

I remember when I thought it quite impossible that the energy in the universe was set up to cater to what Phyllis wanted. But now I'm a fan of the Red Queen.

"I'm just one hundred and one, five
months and a day," said the Queen.
"I can't believe that!" said Alice.
"Can't you?" the Queen said in a pitying
tone. "Try again: draw a long breath,
and shut your eyes."
Alice laughed. "There's no use trying,"
she said: "one *can't* believe impossible
things."
"I daresay you haven't had much
practice," said the Queen. "When I was
your age, I always did it for half-an-
hour a day. Why, sometimes I've
believed as many as six impossible
things before breakfast."

It's no longer impossible for me to believe that some indefinable source draws to me what matches my frequencies. Knowing that I have a strange attractor allows me to operate in the world in a different way. For example, when I get up, if I want chocolate truffles from the universal candy store, I turn my internal dial to 'chocolate truffles' and crank up the volume for a while. Then I stop thinking about them and go on about my day. If I find myself surrounded by lime gummy bears, I just keep on walking, gently holding chocolate truffles in the back of my mind.

It's expecting without yearning. Sort of a Zen thing.

Before I knew about my strange attractor, my way of getting truffles out of my environment was exhausting:

1. Search the Web
2. List candy stores
3. Call them all:
    a. Chocolate truffles? Brand?
    b. Ingredients, please.
    c. Your location? Hours?
4. Go test truffles. But don't buy till I've sampled all, so I'm sure to get the best.

My strange attractor eliminates all that. Whatever truffles show up are the beneficial ones for me because they match my chocolate truffle broadcast.

What does this mean in practical terms? It means that before I do something, I get clear about what results and emotions I want. Then I program my strange attractor with those images and feelings.

Now in my wisdom years, I know the emotions I want and the ones I don't. I don't want poverty or spiritual deprivation, violence or pessimism. Know they exist. Don't choose them.

I just keep putting energy into the ones I want: easy healing; delightful learning; delicious relationships; awesome dancing, beauty and music. And I want creativity that is filled with doing good, making money and having fun. I pay attention to what I do want. The simple act of focusing on it gives it energy. Energy vibrates. Vibrations attract. Use energy to program your strange attractor and guess what shows up?

I have also learned to ignore those things I do not want in my life. Two people can stand in exactly the same spot and have opposite experiences. One looks down, sees litter in the gutter and whines about the pollen. The other looks up, sees purple orchid tree blossoms and fairy dust in the air. You make your choice.

Within the framework of US society, it's all available: the Good, the Bad and the Ugly. Our magnificent self's built-in strange attractor is our touchstone. We can bring into reality the tapestry of our dreams . . . right here in this awesome candy store of the United States.

As Mr. Spock said, we are a most interesting nation to observe. It's even more entertaining to live here. As far as the self is concerned, the candy store is just the drama in the background. Rosa Parks,

Viktor Frankl and Maathai Wangari prove that the self can transcend and transform any distracting dramas.

If you live in Bhutan, the chocolate truffles of happiness are front row center in importance. If you live in the US, you can sample your way through a thousand aisles as you go. Either way, you will get your chocolate truffles if that's what you've programmed into your strange attractor.

(end of *Vision* article)

The strange attractor is among many new ideas in the quantum world. I like to remember what Max Planck said about new ideas.

Max Planck

Max Plank should know about new ideas, being the inventor of quantum theory. If any one person could be given that title, it would be Planck. In 1900 while only 22 years old, he devised the formula that renounced classical physics and introduced the quanta of energy. Max Planck's biography says, "At first the theory met resistance. But due to the successful work of Niels Bohr in

1913 (calculating positions of spectral lines using the theory), it became generally accepted." Planck received the Nobel Prize for Physics in 1918.

Max Planck said,

"A new scientific truth does not succeed

because the opponents are convinced

or (. . .) educated.

However, they die and

the new generations learn about it

from the beginning as the truth."

It's interesting that it took a couple of generations for quantum theory to become accepted. One way for a new truth to take hold is to wait til the Old Guard dies, as Max Planck says. Let the next generation grow up with the truth.

But there's a faster, easier way. It lies in the wisdom of Yoda. It deals with our own power over our own brains using the RAS and the intention to be open to new truths.

"You must
UNLEARN
what you have learned."
-- Yoda

Consciousness in Chaos

I have a confession to make. I don't like chaos. I like order. I like peace. I like tranquility. I'm working on finding a way to stay there. But I know that what my friend Charlie Carson says is true:

In my little world

of peace and tranquility

. . . lurks atrophy!

So I want to stay peaceful in a healthy way, not because I'm sunk in the deadly swamp of denial.

If indeed there is order at the heart of the universe, might it be OK for me to be more in love with order than I am with chaos? Might it be OK for me to want to spend more of my life in an orderly system instead of a chaotic system?

So, how do I stay in an orderly system as much as possible . . . and stay open to, aware of, and processing all incoming information so that I don't atrophy? If I can get out of the Newtonian drag (suffering through long periods of chaos) and increase my periods of tranquility, might that be preferable?

To answer my questions, I went back to the chaos model. Think in terms of the KMC from Chapter 3.

If I get to the explosions point *earlier,* I can avoid some chaos. How do I do that? The system still has to build enough chaotic pressure to shatter the Tolerance Boundary (TB). So perhaps if I *lower* my TB, then the system reaches explosion point earlier at a lower level of chaos.

The interactive "Play" version of this shows the right red dotted line (Equilibrium Scale) moving to the left. As it moves to the left, the TB^{-1} (new Tolerance Boundary) has shrunk closer to the mid-line, sort of

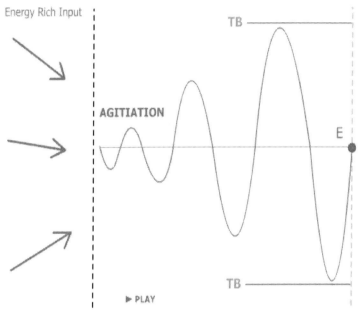

KMC with lowered Tolerance Boundary (TB^{-1})
and therefore less chaos
and smaller explosion

like closing a window. So just before the system explodes (E), there is less chaos in the system.

This must be what they mean when they say, "You can get the message with a feather or a Mack Truck."

Bigger TB = bigger explosion = Mack Truck

Smaller TB = smaller explosion = feather

What does a smaller TB look like? How do I create it? Can I consciously choose to have a lower tolerance for pain in my system? If so, can I lower my pain tolerance (my T.B.) without ignoring or repressing the ERI and getting stuck in Stability? Can I have order without entropy?

A lower TB would come from having an increased awareness of anxiety in my system. Sort of a DEW Line (a Distance Early Warning Line). It would mean: check in with the system more often and more honestly. It would mean: stay alert for any new ERI. Pay attention to how that information affects my system. Ask questions like:

~ Does this information serve me? Is it beneficial?

~ Does it feel good?

~ Does it fit my purpose?

If the answer is "yes", embrace it. That means make room for it, adapt to it and include it.

If the answer is 'no', then there is one more question: Is there something here for me to learn? Tricky question because we humans have blind spots. If your answer is 'no' and there really *is* something that's beneficial for your system to learn, then you've missed a chance to improve the system. But don't worry, the same information will be attracted to you again for the same reason, and you'll get another shot at it.

Ram Dass has been an important wisdom teacher for me. I first met him when I was in high school. Longmont's First Congregational Church brought him to the community for a weekend of talks as part of their Lay-Clergy Institute. He told a story of a college student who went to his yogi looking for an answer to a difficult life choice. The student was deeply in love and wanted to get married. He knew if he got married he would have to give up his advanced studies and promising brilliant career in order to be a responsible husband and father.

"What should I do?" he begged.

The wise yogi said, "It doesn't matter what you choose. Either way, you'll get what you need."

In his book <u>The Only Dance There Is</u>, Ram Dass said it something like this:

> If you don't get the
> lesson the first time
> around, don't worry.
>
> Central Casting will just
> dress up another clown
>
> and put them on your
> doorstep.

You can also decide that the incoming ERI is information that you already know (just wrapped in a different scenario). You have dealt with it before and have a place to put it. If you have no reaction to it, then it won't create any initial waves or feedback. If it doesn't create any agitation, then there won't be any chaos. You walk away from it, knowing that it exists and is not important for your system.

You can buy in to Alarmist Al's fear. . .

Or you can walk away from it,

and let him go look

for another victim to amplify his fear.

Conscious choice allows us to avoid what we don't want in our system. Avoidance is only unhealthy if the information is beneficial for your system. Alarmist Al thrives on negative Twinkies. If you don't, then don't eat Twinkies with him.

Isn't the reaction in the second scene a denial of reality? Yes. Exactly. It's a denial of Alarmist Al's reality. You say, "Been there. Done that. Don't choose it anymore." Remember. Quantum has multiple realities – literally. You not only have the right to choose yours – you have the delight of choosing it.

I've designed some quantum T-shirts for this.

In human systems, the quantum event of transformation can be a result of choices made over a period of time. Your choices create an energetic pattern during the Newtonian cooking time in the chaos cycle. There are two ways that energetic pattern forms. One is by *default*: something happens, you react . . . something happens, you react, etc. The other way a pattern forms is by *choice*: Something happens, you make a choice. . . next thing happens, you make a choice, etc.

The pattern that is made takes effect during the quantum event at the explosion point. A default pattern is more likely to move you into isolation, separation, atrophy. A conscious pattern hedges your bets in favor of higher complexity, inclusion and wholeness.

We all have wake-up calls. They are a natural part of the chaos-order cycle. We can invite our wake-up calls to be delivered by a feather instead of a Mack truck. Stay open, be aware, and make conscious choices.

Many years ago I heard the wisdom of

Change is mandatory,

Pain is optional.

More recently, I have heard the promising harbinger of global healing from Dr. Roger Teel of Denver's Center for Spiritual Living (CSL). He said,

The world has learned

all it can

through struggle.

Dr. Teel is a leader in the Association for Global New Thought (agnt.org) along with Dr. Michael Beckwith, Barbara Marx Hubbard and others. They focus on spiritually guided activism, reflecting the teachings of the world's great spiritual traditions.

It's time to choose new paradigms as we let the old ones starve from lack of attention. The Association for Global New Thought believes:

> ~ that consciousness is infinitely creative;

> ~ that the community of all life is sacred;

> ~ in meditation and healing prayer;

> ~ in reverence and service to humanity and planet earth;

> ~ in compassionate activism based on interfaith and multi-cultural understanding.

A world that works for everyone.

Summary Chapter 5
The Quantum Event

I. The Quantum Milkman

    A. Rapid change of emotions (delight to fear to delight)

    B. Two basic emotional frequencies: fear and love

    C. Strong fear frequencies (Ahmed) overwhelm another person's (Phyllis) love frequencies

    D. Strong love frequencies (Hawa) overwhelm Ahmed's fear frequencies

    E. Understand the system's change of emotional frequencies in terms of both:

        1. Overwhelming a major vibration into a minor status = pushing it down

        2. Magnetizing/entraining a minor vibration into a major vibration = pulling it up

II. The Energetics of a Quantum Event

    A. Definition of a quanta: smallest measurement for unit of movement

    B. Simplified definition of quantum: jump from here to there without covering the ground in between

    C. A "Beam me up, Scottie" type of event

III. Big Picture

    A. Chaos cycle is predictable. The cycle itself is Newtonian.

    B. The explosion point is quantum.

    C. So within the Newtonianly predictable chaos cycle there is a quantum event at explosion point

    D. The quantum event at explosion point either:

        1. Transforms

            ⚔   drops deadwood

            ⚔   adds complex frequencies

            ⚔   adds energy

            ⚔   moves toward wholeness

        2. Disintegrates

            ⚔ looses energy

            ⚔ looses complexity

            ⚔ moves toward isolation, separation, entropy

IV. A Wrinkle in Time

    A. Energy patterns are the history of the system - its memory

    B. Those energy patterns are created by the choices made during the cooking time of the chaos cycle

    C. A skin wrinkle as an example of a cellular memory pattern, also known as a belief

D. New cells nest into old wrinkle pattern because the energetic memory tells them to

V. Change Your Beliefs to Change Your History

A. Beliefs → Actions → History

B. Brain's Reticular Activation System, the RAS

C. RAS is your belief-maker and your belief-breaker

D. RAS screens out overload of sensate information

E. RAS lets in only that which agrees with your beliefs

F. You can reprogram your RAS

G. Tell your RAS to let in more information . . . and mean it

VI. Consciousness

A. Consciousness is awareness of connection to the whole

B. Unified Field Theory

C. Consciousness is the force that unifies gravity, ELM, weak and strong nuclear forces

D. Conscious choice in a living system

    1. Trust-based: I'm OK.

    2. Thoughtful observation: What are the facts? (objective, unemotional)

3. <u>It's about information</u>: There's a message here. What is it?

4. <u>Big system picture</u>: What's happening in the larger system?

5. <u>Responsibility</u>: What's my part of the problem that I can fix?

E. Unconscious reaction in a living system

1. <u>Fear-based</u>: I'm in trouble.

2. <u>Knee-jerk response</u>: Call the police.

3. <u>It's about security</u>: I've got to protect myself.

4. <u>Small system approach</u>: They're after me.

5. <u>Blame</u>: Find the offender and punish them.

E. Your Strange Attractor brings to you what you ask for and focus on. Remember Alice in Chocolate Wonderland.

F. Example of healthy cells and cancer cells

 1. Cancer cells unconscious – not aware of their connection to the whole; isolated behavior kills the host/whole

 2. Healthy cells conscious – monitor their behavior based on benefit to or condition of the host / whole

G. Moving the explosion point in the KMC

 1. Mack truck = moving the point to the right = longer periods of higher chaos before explosion point

 2. Feather = moving the point to the left = shorter periods of lower chaos before the explosion point

 3. Can we get out of the Newtonian drag of suffering through long intense periods of chaos by changing our behavior during the cooking time? Practices that can support the feather:

    a. Stay open to all incoming ERI

    b. Stay aware of the effect

     c. Make choices that enforce the patterns you want

H. The world has learned all it can through suffering. It's time to choose a new paradigm:

A world that works for everyone.

Epilogue
To Third Edition

Having experienced 10 more years of amazing, challenging and deepening life, here's what I want to share.

We are at the beginning of a massive change as a human species. Some call it a paradigm shift, meaning the way we see and experience life will change. I trust this is so. It's about time. It's time to create a world that works for everyone. Bucky Fuller proved mathematically in the 1970's that we have enough to feed, clothe, house, educate and give good water and health to everyone on the earth, now and on-going.

What stands in the way, and what's it got to do with chaos?

In terms of the chaos model, we are at the tolerance boundaries where our existing systems can't hold all the internal dissonance and perturbation. At the explosion points, will we disintegrate or transform? And how can we hedge our bets in favor of transformation?

The one common denominator contributing to disintegration is fear. It makes us rigid. It blocks helpful incoming information. It isolates us from creative solutions. It paralyzes us so we can't respond. It weighs us down so we're ineffective. It confuses our hearing so we can't listen. It narrows our vision so we don't see. It atrophies our hands so we can't reach out. It hardens our hearts so we don't care. Fear kills. It kills us. It kills others. It kills life.

Can we choose to let go of fear as a teacher? Can we insist that we have learned all we can through struggle?

We can and we are. We have the way-showers: Nelson Mandela came out of 27 years in prison and transformed an entire nation without bloodshed. ~ Muhammad Yunus has lifted hundreds of thousands of families out of poverty by creating microfinancing. It's a banking system based on counterintuitive concepts of social collateral and self-governing (not default and punishment). His Grameen/Village Bank has 97% repayment, higher than any other bank. ~ Pope Francis refuses to live in palatial splendor because he represents the soul and spirit of one who walks beside those he serves. These quiet, brilliant iconoclasts are not just appearing in government, finance, and religion. Media has The Daily Optimist, with "solutions news" and now we have One America News Network, with independent credible (non-biased) news casting. Paul Elio says that by 2017 Elio motors will be rebuilding the economy of Shreveport LA as it produces cars with 84 MPG, 5-star safety and a price tag of $6,800 made in the USA . . . a purely American People's Car.

Harvard worked with the Dalai Lama to research brain functioning during meditation. They proved that meditation changes the brain which can be trained/taught to be peaceful, creative, and connective. ~ We have education that focuses on wisdom in addition to knowledge, like Waldorf schools. ~ An Ivy League educated, Wall Street groomed MTV rap star stepped out of the Fast Lane and became a rapper activist. He went to live in Gandhi's ashram in India, created a musical with 16 slum children and performs it globally. His "Empty Hands" CD is free online. http://www.emptyhandsmusic.com/album-gift-for-all/. And the breakthroughs are happening in health & medicine, agriculture and food, clothing, etc., etc., etc. You'll see it everywhere if you know how to look.

And what's the common denominator of these successful r-evolutions? Concern for the whole, respect for the earth and its resources, taking responsibility for the future (aka sustainability), Bucky's More With Less, transparency, creativity, trust, open and receptive attitudes, playfulness ...

So, the first step is "How do I get through fear?"

President Kennedy asked Wernher Von Braun in the early 60's what it would take to get a person to the moon and back safely. Von Braun said, "The will to do it."

For those of you who want to come out of chaos in transformation instead of in disintegration, here's a mantra. If it appeals to you, practice saying it out loud every day.

I choose to use my will to change how I think, how I behave and therefore, my results. I ask for help to do this, and I pay attention. I make welcome and take action on what comes.

*I refuse to accept fear as a
motivator in my life. I choose to
redirect my thoughts, and I invite
others to redirect their thinking. I
choose to look for the good and
celebrate it wherever I see it.*

*I know I can rewire my brain,
abandon old pathways and energize
new pathways.*

*I trust that the world
conspires to support me when my
heart is connected to what I do.*

Thank You.

There are dozens of schools, institutions, life coaches and masters who teach this. To name a few:

Master Teachers: Ram Das, Barbara Marx Hubbard, Martha Beck, Michael Beckwith, Deepak Chopra, Mary Manin Morrissey, Iyanla Vanzant, Joe Dispeza, Don Miguel Ruiz . . .

Programs: Twelve Step groups, The ManKind Project, Landmark/Forum, the Abraham/Hicks materials . .

Centers: Centers for Spiritual Living (CSL), Buddhist retreats, Islamic centers of meditation, Institute of Noetic Sciences, Kripalu, Esalen . . .

Find one and go for it. Get started. Today. Get on your computer and type in the above names and words, and browse. What calls to you?

Ask for what you want:

~ meaningful connection with people

~ deeper communication

~ sense of belonging

~ clearer thinking

~ cleaner health

~ sense of freedom

~ purpose

~ engagement with life

~ joy in simplicity

~ peace

And may your chaos be blessed with transformation.

In trust,
Phyllis Kirk

Palm Desert, California
February 2016

About the Author

I wrote this bio back when I was into impressing people. Although I'm still quite capable of fooling myself, I believe the reason I offer it here is different. I want the reader to know that the material you experience in <u>Quantum Lite</u> comes from a person who has a fairly broad and balanced background, and a very developed left brain.

Phyllis is a humanist, futurist, "recovering" lawyer, writer, speaker, traveler and a mother-sister-aunt-grandmother. She has lived in Germany and Russia. In her fifteen years as a lawyer, she was an attorney for the Solicitor's Office, U.S. Department of Labor, as well as having her own private practice. During three year's living in the Soviet Union, she was the Administrative Director of the multinational joint venture Chadbourne, Hedman, Rabbe and Advocates CCCP and opened the first international joint venture law office in the Soviet Union. She was a partner in ParaGraph, a software programming joint venture of which Gary Kasparov was Vice Chairman. ParaGraph was purchased by Silicon Graphics Inc.

She started her right brain education during her international travels with "Up With People", and has her formal degrees from Illinois Institute of Technology (B.S.), University of Chicago (M.S.T.), University of Denver (J.D.), and a second PhD. (in

Suffering) from Moscow. Her interest in law has broadened beyond traditional legal practice to the more universal aspects of law.

Phyllis's work has been published in *The International Herald Tribune*, *The Systems Thinker*, *Washington Post*, *Komsomolskaya Pravda*, *Moscow News*, and *The Moscow Guardian*. She has been featured in/on *USA Today, NBC, Business in the USSR, Colorado Homes and Lifestyles*. As the keynote speaker for Intercontinental's grand opening of their Moscow palace hotel, the Metropol, her theme was (and still is) how to embrace opportunity in the middle of chaos, and how to be fully human within the human condition.

Moving on from Moscow and lawyering, Phyllis was a corporate trainer in communications and leadership, becoming CEO of the Boulder Center of Accelerative Learning where she worked for 8 years. Then a conscious lifestyle choice took her to live 4 years in the Caribbean and in her heart - both previously unexplored territories. There she created Quantum Lite. For her last career J.O.B., she had the honor of being on staff at The Betty Ford Center as a Spiritual Care Counselor working with people in early addictions recovery. She is now living her chosen reality in the southern California desert, where she is Phyllis-ing one day at a time.

Dr. Ilya Prigogine
Nobel Prize Laureate in Chemistry 1977

Dr. Ilya Prigogine
Nobel Laureate for
Theory of Dissipative Structures

Dr. Ilya Prigogine's Theory of Dissipative Structures is the scientific basis and inspiration for the Kirk Model of Chaos in Chapter 3 of <u>Quantum Lite</u>. The concept of 'Creative Participation in Chaos' comes from his closing comments at The Paradox of Certainty Conference, April 15, 1998: "May your understanding of (chaos theory) make you want to participate in creation." Below are sites where you can read more about Dr. Prigogine.

1. A must-read autobiography of Dr. Prigogine if you want to know the heart of this brilliant man which comes through even when you cannot understand the science he writes about. This autobiography was written at the time he received the Nobel Prize in Chemistry in 1977.

http://nobelprize.org/nobel_prizes/chemistry/laureates/1977/prigogine-autobio.html

2. The Official website of the Nobel Foundations and presentation speech for Dr. Prigogine's Nobel Prize in Chemistry "for his contribution to non-equilibrium thermodynamics, particularly the Theory of Dissipative Structures".

http://nobelprize.org/nobel_izes/chemistry/laureates/1977/presentation-speech.html

3. The International Solvay Institutes for Physics and Chemistry in Belgium where Dr. Prigogine was the Director. (See brief history for a good bio of Dr. Prigogine)

http://www.solvayinstitutes.be/

4. The Ilya Prigogine Center for Studies in Statistical Mechanics and Complex Systems at The University of Texas at Austin, with links to journal articles, and tutorials in chaos physics and other topics.

http://order.ph.utexas.edu/people/Prigogine.htm

Notes

19207804R00130

Printed in Great Britain
by Amazon